This illustrated celebration is the official guide to one of the most influential cultural households of our time: Charleston – the farmhouse in Sussex which was, as a country retreat of the Bloomsbury circle, a hive of painting and writing and whose wonderful surprises can now be enjoyed by the public.

In 1916 Charleston became the home of Vanessa Bell and Duncan Grant, two of Britain's pre-eminent twentieth-century artists and designers. Here, Vanessa raised her children, Julian, Quentin and Angelica, and welcomed such friends as her sister Virginia Woolf and Roger Fry, Maynard Keynes and David Garnett, both of whom were sometime residents. And here, for over fifty years, she and Duncan Grant covered walls, furniture and ceramics with their own decorations. These, along with the works of other artists accumulated through time, form a fascinating collection.

Now painstakingly restored, Charleston is adorned with shades, textures and memories from the past. This delightful book presents the official guide to its rooms by Richard Shone, while Angelica Garnett's reminiscences and explanation of her part in the renovation, Quentin Bell's recollections of the garden, Henrietta Garnett's memoir of her grandmother and the observations of others who stayed in the house provide a vibrant picture of life among one of this century's most famous groups of friends.

Quentin Bell, Angelica Garnett, Henrietta Garnett and Richard Shone are members of the Charleston Trust, which will receive proceeds from this book to help in the continuous task of preserving the house. Should you wish to make a donation, join the Friends of Charleston or have further information, please write to: Alan Martin, The Hon. Secretary, The Charleston Trust, 20A Waldegrave Gardens, Twickenham, Middlesex TW1 4PG, England; or The Royal Oak Foundation, 285 West Broadway, New York, NY 10013, USA.

Charleston, near Firle, about six miles east of Lewes, is open to the public from the beginning of April to the end of October, on Wednesdays, Thursdays, Saturdays, Sundays and Bank Holiday Mondays, 2–6 p.m. (last admission, 5 p.m.). Admission charge £2.50 (1988). No dogs. For the comfort of visitors and to maintain its fabric, numbers within the house are limited. Car parking charge. There is no access for coaches, but alternative arrangements can be made by contacting the Administrator at Charleston Farmhouse, Firle, near Lewes, East Sussex, BN8 6LL – telephone: Ripe (032 183) 265 – between 2.30–5 p.m. on the days the farmhouse is open.

CHARLESTON
Past & Present

Quentin Bell,
Angelica Garnett,
Henrietta Garnett
and
Richard Shone

THE HOGARTH PRESS
LONDON

Published in 1987 by
The Hogarth Press
Chatto & Windus Ltd
30 Bedford Square
London WC1B 3RP

Second impression 1988

British Library Cataloguing in Publication Data

Charleston: past and present. –
(Hogarth lives & letters).
I. Bell, Quentin
942.2'57   DA690.S42/

ISBN 0-7012-0780-9

Acknowledgements for the use of copyright material will
be found on page 6, which is hereby made part of this copyright page.

Photoset in Linotron Baskerville by
Rowland Phototypesetting Ltd
Bury St Edmunds, Suffolk
Printed in Great Britain by
Redwood Burn Ltd
Trowbridge, Wiltshire

CONTENTS

Acknowledgements

The authors wish to thank the following for their kind permission to reproduce copyright material: The Hogarth Press for Virginia Woolf's letter to Vanessa Bell, from *The Letters of Virginia Woolf Volume 2*, © Quentin Bell and Angelica Garnett 1976, the excerpt from *Virginia Woolf: A Biography Volume 2*, © Quentin Bell 1972, the excerpts from *The Diary of Virginia Woolf Volume 3*, © Quentin Bell and Angelica Garnett 1980 and *Volume 5*, © Quentin Bell and Angelica Garnett 1984, and Julian Bell's letter to Vanessa Bell, from *Julian Bell: Essays, Poems and Letters*, © Quentin Bell 1938. The Tate Gallery Archive 8010.8.215 for Vanessa Bell's letter to Roger Fry, 8010.5.1132 for Duncan Grant's letter to Vanessa Bell and 8010.5.25 for Clive Bell's letter to Vanessa Bell. A. P. Watt Ltd on behalf of the executors of the estate of David Garnett for the excerpt from David Garnett's *The Flowers of the Forest*, © David Garnett 1955, and the letter to T. H. White. The estate of John Maynard Keynes for his letter to Mrs Keynes. The Society of Authors on behalf of The Strachey Trust for Lytton Strachey's letter to Carrington, © The Strachey Trust 1987. Mrs Pamela Diamand, Denys Sutton and Chatto & Windus Ltd for Roger Fry's letters to Helen Anrep, from *The Letters of Roger Fry*, © Pamela Diamand 1972. Frances Partridge for the excerpt from her paper given at the Charleston Symposium, © Frances Partridge 1987. Sir Nicholas Henderson and the *Charleston Newsletter* for the excerpt from newsletter no. 2. Sir Edward Playfair and the *Charleston Newsletter* for the excerpt from newsletter no. 8, Chatto & Windus Ltd for the excerpt from *Deceived with Kindness*, © Angelica Garnett 1984.

For the illustrations, thanks are due to the following: Jeremy Quin *1, 7, 10, 25;* Sir Peter Shepheard *2;* Angelica Garnett *3, 4, 9, 28;* Edward Reeves *6, 13, 19;* Collection, The Reader's Digest Association, Inc. *8;* Lucinda Douglas-Menzies *11, 12, 14, 15, 23, 24;* Andrew Graham *16;* Monty Coles *18, 22;* Howard Grey *21* (From *Omega and After: Bloomsbury and the Decorative Arts* by Isabelle Anscombe, Thames and Hudson, 1981); Chris Bowles, Clifton Nurseries *26;* Deborah Gage *27;* The Tate Gallery Archive Vanessa Bell Photographs G.21 *31,* U.48 *34,* A.30 *37,* R.10 *38* and Barbara Bagenal Collection 40 *35;* Giselle Freund *32.* The vignettes at the beginning of each chapter are by Richard Shone and the front and back covers are by Angelica Garnett.

Charleston Preserved

Charleston Preserved? – that might have been a more accurate title, for the struggle is not yet over, and the fate of Charleston Farm House has yet to be decided. Still, a good deal of preservation has, in one way or another, been undertaken; so here is our story, so far.

Duncan Grant, the last survivor of those adults who had settled at Charleston in the autumn of 1916, died in 1978; he was ninety-three. For many years some of us had been wondering what on earth was going to happen to his house when he died. Not that, strictly speaking, it was his house. Charleston had belonged to the Gage family of Firle since time immemorial; it had been let and sub-let; and in 1916 it was refilled with Vanessa Bell, Duncan Grant, David Garnett, servants, dogs, children (including me) and Belgian hares. Clive Bell soon became a regular visitor; Maynard Keynes was another. The many guests who came to the house and the many decorations they found there are discussed on later pages. The many thousands of visitors who have come to the house since it was opened have found in Charleston a monument and a delight. Already in 1978 it appeared that it should in some manner be preserved.

Attempts were made to devise a course of action. There were several conversations between my sister Angelica (who was born at Charleston) and me, and between me and Viscount Gage – like his heirs, he was invariably friendly and helpful, as were

1. Charleston Farmhouse

some other important people whom I approached. But no one was very optimistic. It was clear from the first that Charleston, if it were to be preserved, would have to be preserved in gold. It seemed extremely unlikely that gold would be forthcoming, for the fact of the matter was – and I am here speaking of the time of my earliest endeavours – that very few people cared what became of Charleston. I remember discussing the matter with a colleague in what is now the University of Newcastle-upon-Tyne and we agreed sadly that no one was at all likely to join in an effort to save the house itself. We thought that the best we could hope for was to take some removable panels, doors, and such like, and attempt to house them in the Victoria and Albert Museum.

Duncan Grant, Vanessa Bell, Roger Fry and their followers had gone so completely out of fashion that we could hope for nothing from the press, public bodies, the public at large or the art world. The memory of Bloomsbury, with which Charleston had so close a connection, was at that time a serious drawback: its art was not cherished, therefore the sooner Charleston could be forgotten, the better.

I argued then and, indeed, still argue that aesthetic fashions provide the worst possible basis for a discussion of what is worthy of preservation. Very few of our great monuments have escaped a period during which they were hated and despised: the terms gothic, baroque, rococo, neo-classical and pre-Raphaelite have all been used as terms of abuse and, as a result, we have lost much which, at one time or another, seemed bad, but which would have delighted later generations. An argument based upon prevailing tastes in art reduces itself to the statement: nothing is worth saving except that which I (the advocate of destruction) happen to like at this moment. The fact – and it is a fact – that things which we now hate we may soon come to love is forgotten. But even if we were to grant that the works of art at Charleston are, or at least have become hateful, the mere existence of the place and the irreplaceable nature of the evidence that it provides of a past society is a part of our history, and for that reason alone Charleston should be saved.

But although this argument is one which we ought always to bear in mind, for discussions which involve aesthetic convictions are seldom marked either by tolerance or by reason, it is now less urgently needed in this particular case, for part of it has already come true. The wheel of taste continues to revolve. Duncan Grant, alone amongst his Bloomsbury friends, lived for so long that he began to see himself coming back into fashion. A strong and passionate distaste for Bloomsbury does persist, and, unfortunately, it informs many elderly people who are in a position to influence the course of events. But amongst the younger artists and art historians there is a new attitude: to them, the old quarrels and prejudices are no more than an historical oddity, and they would no sooner take sides in such a matter than they would join in the old disputes concerning Poussin and Rubens. Their seniors enjoyed Bloomsbury-bashing, but there is something ridiculous about 'old unhappy far off things and battles long ago'.

This change in the critical climate made the hope of preserving Charleston seem rather less forlorn. It would no doubt be hard to accomplish but, still, it might be managed. Thus, in about 1979, I felt that something could be done, something ought to be done and, as I began uncomfortably to realise, it ought to be done by me. I had some further conversations with well-disposed people; they were all very kind; everyone seemed to wish us well; everyone, it appeared, was waiting for me to take some positive action; as for me, I was waiting for a miracle.

It came.

It burst through our front door. Electric, dynamic and explosive, it took the form of Deborah Gage, a delightful, intelligent and immensely energetic young woman whose very first words as she blew into our hall were, 'Charleston must be saved.'

Almost at once, so it seemed, things began to happen. A committee came into existence and began to meet in our drawing room. It was composed of such sensible, useful, agreeable, hard-working people that one began to live in an atmosphere of hope. I, who had for many years been on the shelf, found myself in the chair. Leaflets were printed, circulars distributed, patrons approached, a constitution was devised. In April 1980, the Charleston Trust became a registered charity established to purchase, restore and preserve Charleston in perpetuity. Meetings were held, symposia proliferated, first nights were bespoke, articles were written, appeals were launched, the Friends of Charleston were called into being, a journal created. Rising above this tornado of activity, planning, creating, cajoling and invigorating, Debo 'rides in the whirlwind and directs the storm'. The committee was mainly her work and, if for nothing else, I shall always be grateful to her for having brought me in touch with such delightful people. Whether she or the other members ever regret having put me in charge of our activities I do not like to ask. Certainly, I have had moments when I felt decidedly too old for the job. The very friendliness of the atmosphere makes it almost impossible to keep these dear people in any kind of order.

The meeting of any committee is a dreadful thing, particularly if you are in the chair. The agenda lies before you like a badly made chart. It gives hints of the geography of the coming meeting but those hints may be entirely misleading. Even the minutes may conceal hidden rocks, and beyond them lie Scylla and Charybdis. There is the financial report. The chairman must listen to it carefully and, if he can, conceal his complete ineptitude. Then there is the question of architecture: the relationship between architect and client is not always an easy one, however well intentioned. Then there is the question of restoration within the house; and it is not an altogether consoling thought that this, which creates difficulties enough in committee, creates far worse ones on the spot. When we have dealt with those, we shall have to tackle the garden and grounds; we had a wise and generous friend, the late Lila Acheson Wallace (who, with her husband, DeWitt, founded *Reader's Digest*), helping us with the garden. Then there are events: sweepstakes, cinema shows, meetings, junketings of all kinds. And then there is the eternal question which dominates so much of recent British history: how can we secure American intervention? Then there will also be things that are not on the agenda. The chairman must write to the Grand Cham because some lesser cham feels slighted because someone forgot to mention the contribution of Tartary; and then we have decided to print postcards and to sell them, but cannot decide what postcards to print; and suddenly the question of how many people should be admitted simultaneously to any single room in the house has to be discussed and raises a question of principle, which is always the kind of thing that the chairman tries to avoid because when principles are raised discussion is endless; and then we have the chance to buy a valuable picture which really ought to be at Charleston and where can we find the money; also, where can we find door knobs of the correct date for a proper restoration of the interior, and what *is* the correct date? An insoluble question. And far, far in the distance seems that ever-receding moment when the committee meeting will become a lunch party and we may forget all our disagreements and insoluble difficulties and I can cease in any active way to be a chairman.

But, of course, our real trouble is fund raising. We began by composing an appeal, as eloquent as we could make it. We printed hundreds of copies and sent them out to all the captains of industry whose secretaries, I imagine, put them straight into the waste-paper basket. Then there was a bigger, better, glossier appeal signed, I seem to remember, by the chairman himself – and a few of these did, I believe, actually elicit a reply: it is interesting to see how many different ways there are of saying no. But we have, in fact, raised £800,000. A surprising proportion of that money has been donated in small subscriptions by people who are enthusiastic about Charleston and Bloomsbury and who though poor in fortune, are rich in generosity. Such are the Friends of Charleston, of whom there are about two thousand.

It was thanks to this popular response and some valuable gifts that we were able to purchase the house. How splendid it would have been if at that point we could have handed it over to the National Trust. That body had indeed taken a careful look at the premises and had liked what it had seen. But the National Trust is, of necessity, a hard-headed suitor. It agreed that Charleston was sufficiently charming, but made it clear that the bride would have to bring an enormous dowry.

Such misgivings were, at the time, understandable, and partly shared by the Charleston Trust itself. During his last years, Duncan had lived almost entirely in his studio; the walls were damp, the roof leaked, but it was habitable and, thanks to a large stove, it was one of the few rooms in the house which was not very cold; but outside the studio terrible things were happening. When Grace Higgens – our treasure and our friend – came to the end of her enormous energy and ceased to wage her long battle against dirt and decay (I am glad to say that she had some years of rest in a very snug little house) there came a period of shifts and expedients. Although some valiant efforts were made to continue her brave defensive action, it was by then a losing battle. Charleston had always been a cold, damp house, but now water was pouring in all over the place; the decorated wall surfaces mouldered, the painted woodwork began to serve a vast population of pests, the pictures decayed and, where they were painted on three-ply, became alive with woodworm, fabrics crumbled. While outside in the garden, the considerable concourse of plaster figures melted beneath the autumn rains, froze and cracked in the winter's frosts, and in the summer were buried beneath a jungle of weeds.

In the old days, when decorations began to show wear and tear, the artists happily painted over them with a new design. Restoration or conservation seemed too dull a solution; it was much more fun to invent something new and change the entire aspect of a room; pictures were sold to meet the increasing cost of living, but they could be copied or replaced. The rooms were always changing, the decorated ones the scene of continual experiments in design; there was no attempt to produce a permanent monument and the idea of conservation never entered the heads of the artists. *Après nous le déluge*; indeed, the deluge was already visible in the cellar and elsewhere.

The committee had to find an architect experienced in the art of saving ancient buildings and ready to make the house waterproof. Heroic measures were set afoot. One day passers-by were startled to see the skull and crossbones pinned to every door and notices couched in terribly imperative language forbidding entry. The entire house had been filled with poison gas – a vapour so penetrating and so lethal that it would kill every beetle, bug, worm, fungus, mould or mouse in the place. The roof was then removed and replaced, and after that a great many other steps were taken to make Charleston dry, solid and permanent. But this task was made more arduous by reason of the fact that, both inside and out, there were precious, friable works of art and these – it was the whole object of the operation – had somehow to be preserved.

The work of the architects and builders is complex, incomprehensible, appallingly expensive and never ending. Years pass and still somehow there is work that needs to be done or redone. But the work of the restorer, although less incomprehensible, seems even more difficult, complex, expensive and endless. The task of consolidating and stabilising the house and its contents requires – as our restorers at Charleston have shown – extreme sensitivity and patience, and painstaking skill. Consider what would appear a simple matter: imagine a wall that was once green and must again be painted green. For a very long time no painting can be done: the wall is damp, it must be insulated from the damp, then it must be plastered. That may sound simple, but the plaster must be of a special kind, it must be bound with goat's hair. Does anyone still make such plaster? In the end it is discovered that someone does. But then the plaster must have time to dry out, and this may take a couple of years. Then, when all seems ready, it is necessary to take up a great part of the plaster in order to install a radiator, also an electric light fitting is needed in the corner, and when these works are finished someone suggests that the electric light plug should be of the original type. Ages have passed, and still we have not painted the wall green. But at last the surface is ready. It would take too long to describe our struggles to arrive at the correct colour, for let no one suppose that the restorers slapped on the colour without due thought – they worked very carefully, often with samples of the original hue; but one must remember that paint over a large area can take on a different look and then the light at Charleston – a beautiful light – is very changeable, and so the reflected changes and counterchanges are inevitable. It is not inevitable that, when we have at last found a solution, and when the wall has been made to look like a Charleston wall (that is to say, very badly painted, with every brush stroke showing), and when it has been 'distressed' (i.e. banged about to save it from looking too new), some fiend should appear with a photograph which shows that the wall was not green, but pink. Such things do happen, for we are trying to arrive at the original colour of a house with the varying tints of an aged chameleon. At some point we have to decide what looks best, what was most characteristic.

(Need I add that when all these decisions have been made and all these operations performed, an insurance man turns up and says that it will be necessary to take up the wall in order to install a smoke detector . . .)

We laugh that we may not weep, and there have certainly been moments during the history of the restoration of Charleston when laughter seemed the only answer to fate's unkindness. But I would hate anyone to think that our troubles have engendered a frivolous attitude or that our doubts and difficulties have not been considered in a very serious spirit. The experts who have done the practical work have applied themselves cautiously and conscientiously to what has been called 'one of the most difficult and imaginative feats of restoration current in Britain'.

There are others amongst us who, while maintaining a sympathetic attitude to the manifold perplexities of these craftsmen, have to bear in mind the desperate need for economy. As our problems multiply, so do our liabilities. Every change has to be considered with our expenditure in mind. Our funds melt away with alarming rapidity. Nor, when all the rooms have resumed their former aspect and when the house is sound, and the garden restored to its glory, will our troubles be over. A house that is devoted to the public must be guarded, tended and kept in good repair. And so, in addition to the ordinary responsibilities of the householder, we must employ guardians, guides and gardeners. Moreover, and most important of all, we have to find an endowment sufficient to resist the progress of inflation. At the time of writing, these demands are formidable and we do not yet know how we are going to meet them. I think that the trustees may be justly proud of what they have done so far, but the question mark with which I began remains.

Quentin Bell, Christmas 1986

RICHARD SHONE

Official Guide to the House and Garden

Introduction

A visitor to Charleston, approaching the house by the lane from the main road, may be surprised that so agricultural a landscape should be the setting for a house associated with a celebrated district of London. But Charleston had long been part of a busy network of farms. It belonged to an area of mixed farming, of root crops and grain, of dairy and, above all, sheep farming. Until purchased by the Charleston Trust in 1981, it formed part of the Firle estate owned by the Gage family, inhabitants for centuries of nearby Firle Place. It is not known exactly when Charleston was erected but a late sixteenth-century frame structure was revealed during recent restoration, at the house's north-east corner. Most of Charleston, however, dates from the late seventeenth and early eighteenth centuries, with minor twentieth-century additions. It is a typical Sussex vernacular house, composed of many different materials but principally of brick and flint, built, like several neighbouring houses, for farmers working the estate, the labourers and their families living in outlying cottages. But by the 1900s, with improved farming methods and increased mechanisation, so many tenant farmers were not necessary to the running of the estate and their houses began to be leased to outsiders.

For several years at the beginning of the century (and probably until 1914), two sisters had run a summer boarding house at

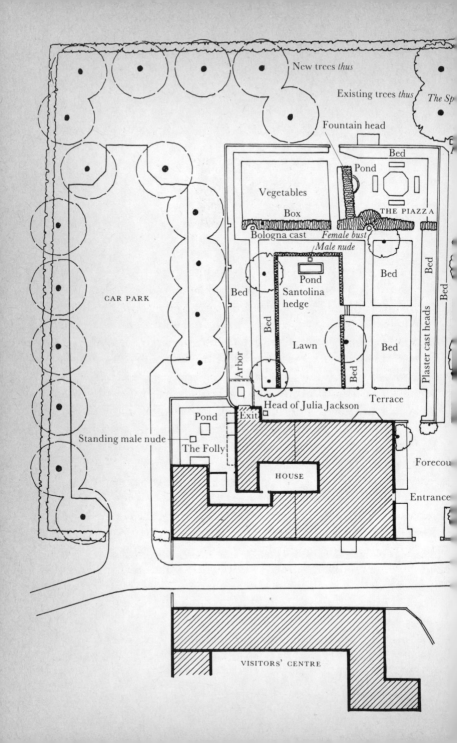

New trees *thus*

Existing trees *thus*   *The Sp*

Fountain head

Bed

Pond

Vegetables

Box

THE PIAZZA

Bologna cast   *Female bust*

Male nude

Bed

Pond

Bed

Bed

Santolina
hedge

CAR PARK

Bed

Lawn

Bed

Bed

Arbor

Bed

Terrace

Head of Julia Jackson

Exit

Pond

Standing male nude

The Folly

HOUSE

Forecou

Entrance

Plaster cast heads

Bed

VISITORS' CENTRE

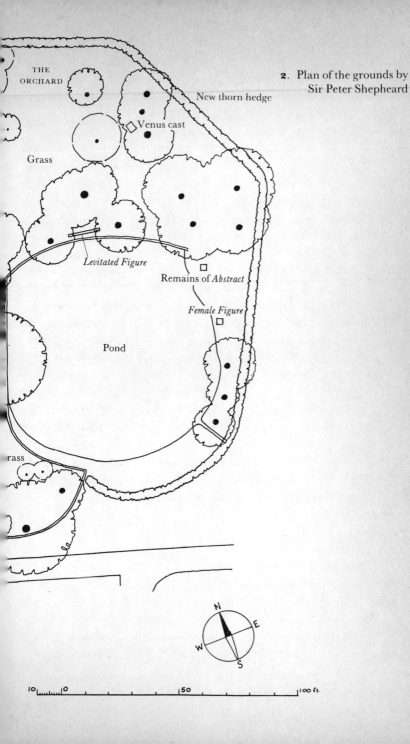

THE ORCHARD

New thorn hedge

Venus cast

Grass

Levitated Figure

Remains of *Abstract*

Female Figure

Pond

Grass

2. Plan of the grounds by
Sir Peter Shepheard

10 ⌊ᴜ⌊ᴜ⌊ᴜ 0   50   100 ft.

Charleston with bedrooms on the first and second floors, leaving china number plates on their doors (still in place) and expanses of genteel wallpaper as reminders of this brief commercial phase. A well-known local man, Mr Stacey, who leased the property with other neighbouring farms, then sub-let the house to some neglectful tenants, the Rays. When Leonard Woolf, living nearby, looked over Charleston in May 1916, his wife, Virginia Woolf, reported his impressions in a letter of the 14th to her sister Vanessa Bell: 'it is used apparently as a weekend place, by a couple who keep innumerable animals, and most of the rooms are used by animals only.' Mr Stacey welcomed the opportunity to cancel this arrangement and it was thus generally known in the district that Charleston was once more to let.

By the autumn of 1916, Vanessa Bell was resolved to leave Wissett Lodge in Suffolk where she had been living for several months with Duncan Grant, David Garnett and her two sons, Julian and Quentin. As conscientious objectors, the former two had eventually been exempted from military service as long as they continued to work on the land. At Wissett Lodge, they were self-employed and this, under the terms of their exemption, did not constitute work of 'national importance'. Vanessa therefore decided to move to Sussex, to a district she knew well, having stayed often in Firle and at Asham House, still leased by the Woolfs. In September 1916 she, having found work on a neighbouring farm for Duncan and Bunny Garnett, rented Charleston from Mr Stacey and moved her family there in October.

Virginia Woolf had intimated to her sister that Charleston lacked some amenities and needed doing up 'but you could make it lovely'. That the house itself was in a way primitive (no electricity or telephone and cold water only in the bathroom) was, in a sense, part of its attraction. Wissett Lodge, which was furnished, had had to be left in good order for the next tenants (and Vanessa's and Duncan's murals whitewashed before they left); Charleston was a bare canvas; and where Wissett was in a village, with prying and sometimes disapproving neighbours, Charleston was comparatively remote, reached through fields by an unmade track half a mile from the quiet Lewes–Eastbourne road.

The first three years in the house were often uncomfortable and difficult. To Vanessa fell the problems of feeding and looking after a large household during a period of shortages. Servants, used to the bustle of town-life, were difficult to attract, and they came and went at an alarming rate. Water had to be hand-pumped each afternoon (the supply shared with Mr Stacey for use on the farm); earth-closets had to be emptied, oil lamps prepared, fires lit and tended in icy rooms (the winter of 1916–17 was particularly harsh). Getting to and from the house required considerable planning. Walking from Glynde station with Clive Bell, Molly MacCarthy thought the prospect of Charleston across damp and misty fields was the nearest thing she had encountered to Wuthering Heights.*

In spite of such conditions, visitors swelled the household, bringing welcome news and gossip from London, toys and chocolate for the children. Clive Bell and Mary Hutchinson, Roger Fry, Lytton Strachey and, above all, Maynard Keynes were regular guests. They brought change and relief from the sometimes tense atmosphere which developed as the war continued. Bunny could become irritable and explosive, Duncan taciturn and, later, seriously unwell. Vanessa, 'cut off', as she wrote to Virginia in February 1918, from painting which was her 'principal occupation', felt tetchy and off balance. As a result, even her intimate friendship with Roger Fry suffered when he came to stay close by in the summer of 1918. In the same year, intermittent poor health was compounded by her pregnancy. The crisis came following the birth of her and Duncan's daughter on Christmas Day, 1918; the baby, Angelica, refused to thrive and there were further appalling problems with servants. It was a long time

* Duncan Grant, in conversation with the author, *c.* 1972.

before Vanessa could rid her memory of these anxious and sometimes despondent months in spite of her enormous pleasure at
the birth of her daughter; it had been, she recalled, the 'most
awful time' of her life.

Later in 1919 Vanessa and her household returned to London,
although Charleston was retained. In the early 1920s, the lease
of the house secured, she set about making it less ramshackle, a
more comfortable and more attractive place to spend holidays
and long periods in which she and Duncan could paint, away
from the distractions of London. Charleston came to be used
during the children's holidays from school and for occasional
week-ends. Improvements gradually accrued. The greatest addition to the house was the building of a large studio in 1925,
designed by Roger Fry in collaboration with the artists. (Until
then, they had used rooms in the house or an old army hut in the
paddock.) At about the same time some temperamental radiators
were installed (a hot water boiler had been put in in 1919); and
in 1933 electricity was laid on, marked by the gift from Virginia
of two enormous electric fires.

With the approach of another war in 1939, further structural
alterations were carried out with the idea that a country life would
be better than one spent in London. An attic bedroom was
converted into a studio for Vanessa with a large new window
looking over the walled garden and north across the countryside.
The ground-floor dairy next to the studio became Vanessa's
bedroom with French windows onto the garden; her previous
bedroom upstairs became Clive's library with a new bathroom
next to it. For the housekeeper Grace Higgens and her family, a
small sitting room was created between the kitchen and wash
house; and an old chicken house was replaced by a pottery for
Quentin. Finally, the telephone was added just before the war.

During the early years of Vanessa's tenancy, the furnishing of
Charleston had been sketchy and improvised. What the house
may have lacked in comfort or luxury ('One has the feeling of

living on the brink of a move,' wrote Virginia in her diary on 5 March 1919, after a visit) was soon made up for by pictures and books, and striking decorations by Vanessa and Duncan on walls, doors and furniture. Of the first years at Charleston Bunny Garnett was to write in *The Flowers of the Forest* (1955), 'One after another the rooms were decorated and altered almost out of recognition as the bodies of the saved are said to be glorified after the resurrection.'

But before the painters could turn their attention to the embellishment of the rooms, a good deal of furniture had to be found for residents, guests and servants. At first, some was sent down from 46 Gordon Square and several beds from Asham House were conveyed by cart along the Lewes road. Other pieces came second-hand: 'Vanessa and Duncan went searching Lewes and perhaps Brighton for furniture and bought extraordinary things . . . The best find was from Brighton. Cross stitch and bead work chairs . . .'* From the Omega Workshops came dining chairs, a dinner service, a painted table and a chest of drawers; later on, from a house sale in Gordon Square in 1925, Duncan bought two large corner cupboards, a black horsehair sofa and a clutch of chairs; several pieces of furniture came from France, of good Provençal workmanship, bought when Vanessa was at La Bergère, the house she kept from 1928–39 near Cassis, among them her writing desk and Duncan's chest of drawers for his bedroom. In 1939, much of Clive's furniture from his flat in 50 Gordon Square was installed, including his large decorated bookcase and six Venetian chairs.

All these disparate objects were made harmonious within the rooms by the personal range of colour evolved by the artists in their decorations, as much as by their choice of fabrics for curtains and chairs. Initially, few rooms were conceived as decorative units, the exceptions being Vanessa's bedroom (now the library) and the two doors and fireplace in Duncan's bedroom. In later years, the spare

* David Garnett, in a letter to the author, 19 January 1981.

3. *Self portrait, c.* 1958, Vanessa Bell,
now hanging in the garden room

room (1936) and the garden room (1945) were decorated with an eye to the whole effect, particular colours running through each scheme. The hall and passages were left unadorned much as they are today, to emphasise the richness of the interiors disclosed at the opening of each door.

The often repeated statement that Duncan and Vanessa covered everything in the house with their work is visibly untrue. Many pieces of furniture remained plain, the walls of several rooms were left a single colour and of the dozen or more main doors in the house only five were decorated. The bedroom known as Maynard Keynes's room, for example, is completely free of decorative features, save for a stained glass panel in the door. At the same time, it should be emphasised that even when walls were painted white or a simple plain colour, the tone and texture were always carefully considered.

Charleston is the only surviving example of Vanessa's and Duncan's domestic decoration and, as such, is a rich repository of their style and method of design, but there is no equivalent in the house

4. *Self portrait, c.* 1910, Duncan Grant, now hanging in
Vanessa Bell's bedroom

of the often grander schemes which they carried out elsewhere. The fact that Charleston was a rented house and for many years only used for holidays perhaps accounts for this. It has an air of genial and haphazard improvisation, done when the spirit moved and over a long period. Fortunately for us, we can now see the gradual transformation of the artists' approach to decoration over half a century. Without it jarring we can move from the sharply accented colour of Duncan's early linen chest and library door to the ample, flowing treatment of the overmantel in the garden room; from the simplicity of Vanessa's flowers below the window in Clive's study (*c.* 1917) to the more elaborate ease of her kitchen-cupboard panels of *c.* 1950, almost her last substantial decoration for the house.

Special to the atmosphere and complex visual impression of the rooms at Charleston were the numbers of pictures hanging there. Most were by the Charleston artists themselves, their immediate family and friends. But in 1939 the house was greatly enriched by the arrival of Clive's French pictures and those from Vanessa's and Duncan's studios in London. Some of the best, such as those by

Picasso, Gris and Vlaminck, had been bought before the First World War when Clive and Roger Fry had championed the Post-Impressionists and their successors; others came as gifts from Clive's French friends such as Derain and Segonzac; a little Matisse, which hung in the garden room, was bequeathed to Vanessa by Roger Fry in 1934. All were hung in the house alongside paintings and drawings by Delacroix and Modigliani, Watts and Sickert, Pasmore and Coldstream. Among the sculpture was the bust of Coco by Renoir, the Chinese Goddess of Mercy in the studio, heads by Gimond and Tomlin. There were paintings by Vanessa's and Duncan's colleagues in the London Artists' Association; water colours of Burma by a Grant family forebear, anonymous works in wool and on glass, and a large classical landscape bought by Duncan in Paris and which later turned out to be by Poussin. (For a fuller account of the Charleston pictures and of the Poussin, see articles in the *Charleston Newsletter*, 1986, nos. 16 and 17.)

A visitor to Charleston cannot fail to notice the large quantity of books in the house and the presence of writing tables, inkpots and desks. Although painting was the main activity of the household (with Quentin and Angelica taking to it from an early age), writing and reading occupied all its inhabitants. Most of the books still in the house (for many have been dispersed) are the legacy of, above all, Clive Bell. His impressive library included considerable collections of English, French and classical literature (the last from his Cambridge days), many in fine editions or eighteenth-century bindings – Voltaire, Gibbon, Walpole, Pepys, Byron – and innumerable paperback editions of French history, belles-lettres and fiction. In fact, contemporary French fiction seems to have been more widely read by the household than was English: little by Greene or Waugh, Isherwood or Bowen, for example, but plenty by Colette, Mauriac, Giraudoux, Giono, Sartre and Camus. Many of Clive's art books – often sent as review copies – and exhibition catalogues are to be seen in his downstairs study.

Clive's sons, Julian (to whom the collection of English poetry in the house largely belonged) and Quentin, were great readers, particularly of history and contemporary politics. The painters were more reluctant readers, Virginia Woolf regarding them teasingly as practically illiterate. Vanessa kept her books in her studio at the top of the house – Virginia's works, still in the jackets that Vanessa had designed for them, a few volumes on painting, often from her student days, such as the pocket *Gainsborough* in the Popular Library monographs from Duckworth, her half-brother's firm; volumes of E. M. Forster (her favourite writer, she once told Duncan), children's books, gardening manuals and copies of Thackeray and Charlotte M. Yonge, which she would read to her grandchildren. Duncan's books, kept in his dressing room and in the studio, again included much French literature (such as presentation copies from Gide, Copeau and Cocteau), books by his friends from early Bloomsbury days, travel guides, louche novels and several well-read favourites such as Ackerley's *Hindoo Holiday*, Mrs Smith's *Memoirs of a Highland Lady*, a set of Jane Austen, and Russian fiction – Aksakov, Turgenev and Tchekov, often in Constance Garnett's translations.

The painters were less careful with their books than Clive. While he liked to keep his in good order, Duncan and Vanessa would use theirs in still lifes or in portraits, leaving them about the studio for months to become smudged with paint, their jackets torn, covers ringed from cups and glasses. Only a fastidious bibliophile such as Cyril Connolly, who lived nearby in later years and often came to talk books with Clive, would deplore their condition, not least the candle-greased copy of Eliot's *The Waste Land*, a rare first edition from The Hogarth Press.

The peace and domestic routine of the house ensured uninterrupted hours for writing. Clive wrote several books here including parts of *Civilization* and his memoir *Old Friends* (1956); Julian wrote many of his poems such as those in his book *Winter Movement* (1930); and Quentin, an unpublished history of Monaco and his first published work *On Human Finery* (1947). Before he became famous with his

Lady into Fox (1921), David Garnett wrote a pseudonymous novel, *Dope Darling*, and several local stories he heard when working in the area as a farm labourer found a place in some of his later fiction. But the most celebrated book composed in the house is Maynard Keynes's brilliant polemic *The Economic Consequences of the Peace*, most of which was written in his bedroom in August and September 1919. Several of those now invaluable papers read to the Memoir Club were also written here, including Vanessa's memoir of her sister's childhood and Duncan's of the Cambridge Apostles of his youth. And, of course, thousands of letters were sent and received; Vanessa was an assiduous letter-writer, given to comic accounts of Charleston life, and Clive kept up a voluminous correspondence with his friends. Eagerly awaited was the arrival each morning of the postman at Charleston, bringing, perhaps, hilarious letters from Virginia to Vanessa, accounts of motoring catastrophes from Roger Fry and begging letters to Duncan from impecunious friends.

While the house gradually assumed the character we can recognise today, the garden, too, underwent a transformation. When Vanessa and her family moved to Charleston, the walled garden was mainly given over to vegetables and fruit trees and the orchard and paddock were neglected. Over the following years, much was achieved under Vanessa's and Duncan's increasing enthusiasm for gardening and their taste for strong colours and profusely filled flowerbeds. Paths and a gravelled terrace were planned (Duncan responsible for the latter); the lawn was made with a small tile-edged pool at one end; a mosaic laid and statuary introduced. Though the painters themselves worked in the garden (and Maynard Keynes, in early years, weeded the paths), gardeners were also employed, notably a local man, Eric Stevens. With Vanessa fully resident at Charleston from 1939, she was able to supervise the garden's progress more closely and it is to the period of the Second World War that its most intense cultivation belongs. Vegetables and fruit were abundant and so many new flowers and shrubs were planted that by the end of the war Vanessa was complaining in a letter to her daughter that 'one can hardly walk down the paths for the plants that get in the way.' Shortly afterwards 'young Mr Stevens' (so called because, although he was a pensioner, his mother was nearly a hundred) was engaged as gardener and a semblance of control was maintained. In 1946 a last important feature was added, the Piazza, an area of mosaic and broken crockery in a corner of the garden. To one side was added a small semi-circular pool with a ceramic mask spouting water (conveyed from the house under the lawn). It provides a charming Mediterranean surprise seen across a deep box hedge (moved there in 1933 from outside the walled garden) which separates it from the main flowerbeds and lawn.

Although Vanessa's was the presiding spirit of the garden, Duncan's contribution was important and his letters to Vanessa and his mother make constant mention of seed catalogues, planting and visits to nurseries. He made valiant efforts to remove a creeper from the front of the house; placed the mill-stones along the terrace and plaster-cast heads along the wall; and he planned the small enclosed space outside his studio with its pool, vine and figs, known as Grant's Folly.

It was only in later years that Duncan painted in the walled garden; earlier, he had preferred the pond and barns and was happy to venture with his easel into cowsheds, rickyards and the countryside beyond. Vanessa, on the other hand, was increasingly drawn to the garden; she was rarely content, as she wrote to Roger Fry on 16 September 1921, to paint 'anything I don't find at my door'. When seen together, her paintings of the garden from the 1920s onwards form a visual diary of its progress – the gradual filling of herbaceous borders, the growth of trees and climbing plants on the walls, the changing aspects of the pool in the lawn or the garden, when viewed from an upper window becoming like an oasis, with fields and undergrowth encroaching on all sides. She did not limit herself to the summer season and there are several paintings of the garden under snow in which her sureness of tone and clarity of design lead her to an oriental delicacy. And when weather prevented working out of doors, there were always cut flowers to paint – roses above all, poppies, iris, dahlias, hydrangeas – placed in terracotta or improbable Victorian vases or in pots decorated by Vanessa herself.

If descriptions of life at Charleston and the many photographs taken there by Vanessa evoke an unbuttoned and light-hearted atmosphere, it is because between the wars Charleston remained a home for holidays. Its main periods of occupation were August and September with shorter periods in the spring, at Christmas and the New Year. When they were grown up, Julian and Quentin Bell liked to spend more time there, especially in the winter months. Very occasionally the house was let to outsiders for short spells, to the Penroses and to Herbert Read and his family. Vanessa and Duncan and the three children were Charleston's principal residents, often accompanied by Clive. Bunny Garnett had left in 1919 and the frequent stays of Maynard Keynes came to an end with his marriage in 1925 to Lydia Lopokova and their move to nearby Tilton House. The most constant guests were Roger Fry, Lytton Strachey (usually in September of each year), Desmond and Molly MacCarthy; and particular friends of Clive who regularly came were Raymond Mortimer, Francis Birrell and Frances Partridge. Also often invited were Janie Bussy, everyone's favourite and a second cousin of Duncan; the sculptor Stephen Tomlin; Roger Fry's companion Helen Anrep; and the writer and translator Angus Davidson. Among the painters who visited were Edward Wolfe, Robert Medley, George Bergen, Simon Bussy and, in later years, Edward Le Bas. Less frequent guests were E. M. Forster (who first visited in 1919), Mary Hutchinson, several members of the Strachey family and Saxon Sydney-Turner. Companions for the children during holidays would fit easily into the household, such as Barbara Bagenal's daughter Judith, the MacCarthy children, Eve Younger and Nicholas Henderson. Later friends of Julian and Quentin who would stay were Edward Playfair, Anthony Blunt and John Lehmann. If the Woolfs were at Asham or later at Monks House, or the Keyneses at Tilton, they might bring their guests for tea or dinner, such as William Plomer, T. S. Eliot, Frederick Ashton and Dame Ethel Smyth. Occasional visitors in later years included Benjamin Britten and Peter Pears, Peggy Ashcroft, Kenneth and Jane Clark and the painter John Nash. Not all visitors, however, were as welcome as these and in later years Vanessa would contrive excuses to put off visits even from old friends. But she greatly enjoyed having her family to stay; Angelica's four daughters – two at a time – were often there; and after Quentin married Olivier Popham in 1952, he and his family would spend several weeks there each year during university vacations. After the deaths of Vanessa and Clive (in 1961 and 1964 respectively), Duncan continued to entertain visitors, often to luncheon or tea, when a sometimes surprising variety of family, guests and children would crowd elbow to elbow round the circular, painted table. This continued almost to his death in 1978.

In order to run such a hospitable household, Vanessa naturally needed the help of others. In the very early years a disastrous series of servants, dirty, thieving and rude, nearly defeated her. 'Only later, by the grace of God came Grace.'* Grace Germany, having worked for Vanessa in various capacities from the age of sixteen, became housekeeper at Charleston in 1935. She lived there with her husband, Walter Higgens, who was later to help in the garden, and their son, John, and remained as cook and housekeeper until 1970, beloved of family and friends. As a girl, her looks were greatly admired by the painters, so much so that Duncan, seeing her once on the Lewes bus, thought she was the image of Lady Diana Cooper. She sat to the painters on several occasions and appears in Vanessa's large *The kitchen* (1943) now hanging at Charleston.

Over the last few years, as the painstaking restoration of Charleston has been taking place, appreciation of the work of Vanessa

---

* David Garnett, in a letter to the author, 19 January 1981.

Bell and Duncan Grant has greatly increased. Naturally, this has encouraged those people involved in the saving of a house that occupies a conspicuous role in the cultural history of England in the twentieth century. Although principally remarkable for its decorations and pictures, Charleston encapsulates a particular and unusual way of life. It formed the easy and intimate setting for decades of hard work and was the meeting place of men and women who were distinguished in a variety of ways from painting and literature to economics, aesthetics and political thought. The beauty of the house and its surroundings is the most striking aspect of Charleston's impact today and the prime reason for saving for future generations its complex visual eloquence. But a visitor should keep in mind that Charleston was also a family home with all its attendant moments of pleasure and sorrow, full of the comings and goings of family and friends, of work and relaxation, of lives lived fully and creatively. It was rarely without the sound of children's voices, of music from the gramophone or Angelica's singing, of gentle conversation from the studio, or the movement of a figure in the garden glimpsed from an upper window. It was a house of schemes and events, of holiday theatricals or Vanessa's school, of the too-brief saga of Duncan's gazebo, of sinking punts and temperamental cars, the busy personal lives of family dogs and cats, of ceaseless schemes to combat winter cold. In summer, drifts of laughter came through the open doors, cigar smoke curling into the air against the flint walls; and, as Virginia Woolf remembered, there was the splashing of fish in the pond, nightingales and the tapping of white roses against a window pane. Charleston was, like all houses, subject to chance and change. This delicate balance of physical object, mood and human values is the key to recapturing its atmosphere and the foundation of its claims on posterity.

The Rooms and their Contents

The following guide gives a brief account of the principal rooms at Charleston, their decorative features and contents, as they exist in 1988. The rooms are listed as you see them on the Visitor's Route around the house and each is introduced by general remarks on its history and function; its contents and pictures are noted clockwise, starting to the left of the room's main door – and, unless otherwise stated, these have been given to the Charleston Trust by Angelica Garnett and Quentin Bell and members of their respective families. Objects illustrated in the photographs relating to that room are denoted thus †. (Details in the photographs may differ from those in the rooms.) Visitors will realise that many of the objects and surfaces are fragile, unique and irreplaceable and are entreated not to touch them – especially the walls and one or two other pieces which are painted with natural pigment and size and will therefore rub off when brushed against. It would have been impracticable to list every item, particularly the numerous pieces of pottery and smaller pieces of furniture. All the pictures, however, have been catalogued (and are in oil, unless otherwise stated); and notes about each artist may be found in the biographical notes, unless they have already been given here. The main sources for information in the guide have been the letters of Vanessa Bell to Roger Fry, Maynard Keynes, Duncan Grant and Clive Bell; Duncan Grant's letters to Vanessa Bell and his mother Ethel Grant; Christopher Mason's film *Duncan Grant at Charleston*; several books listed in the bibliography, especially Angelica Gar-

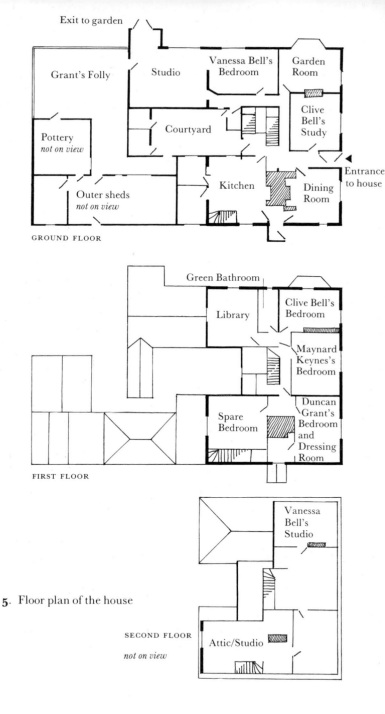

5. Floor plan of the house

nett's *Deceived with Kindness*, Frances Spalding's *Vanessa Bell* and the second volume of David Garnett's autobiography, *The Flowers of the Forest*. Further details have been gleaned from the following people to whom I here offer my thanks: Olivier and Quentin Bell, Nicholas Cann, Deborah Gage, Angelica Garnett, Peter Miall, Richard Morphet and Vicki Walton.

Clive Bell's Study

This room contains some of the earliest decorations to the house. It appears to have served various functions to begin with, notably as a schoolroom for Julian and Quentin Bell and their governess Mrs Brereton (in residence 1918–19) and later as a writing room. In 1939 most of Clive Bell's library of art books and catalogues came here as well as topographical volumes and Julian Bell's books of poetry and literary criticism (to the left of the door as you face it).

The decoration on the upper panel of the door† is by Duncan Grant *c*. 1917. It incorporates an Italian jug containing Omega Workshops paper flowers and a view of the farm from the small window in the dining room. The patterned border below the jug is a transcription of some of the wallpaper of the room as it was in 1916; a portion of it was uncovered during recent restoration. Another version, on canvas and entitled *Paper flowers*, is in the Keynes collection, King's College, Cambridge. The lower panel, replacing a damaged earlier work, is also by Grant, painted in 1958 from a water-colour study he had made of an acrobat. The window decorations are by Vanessa Bell *c*. 1916–17 and the fireplace also by her *c*. 1925–30. The walls were distempered green by Nerissa Garnett under Duncan Grant's direction in *c*. 1970.

In later years the room was most frequently used by Clive Bell, his writing materials and manuscripts being kept in the large French cupboard and in the table drawer; some of his memoir *Old Friends* (1956) was composed here.

CONTENTS

Marquetry centre table, early nineteenth-century, in the Dutch
 style; a wedding present to Clive and Vanessa Bell, 1907

French walnut armchair, *c*.1700, upholstered in fabric *West Wind*,
 designed by Duncan Grant for Allan Walton Ltd, 1931; reproduction by Laura Ashley, 1987

Armchair upholstered in *Abstract*, designed by Vanessa Bell for
 Allan Walton Ltd, 1931; reproduction by Laura Ashley, 1987

Table with tiles, *c*.1930, designed by Duncan Grant and made by
 Kallenborn

Figurines and pottery by Quentin Bell including the centre
 lampshade

On the cupboard: *Head of Hermes*, weathered plaster cast from the
 garden wall

PICTURES

Landscape, 1921, Keith Baynes

Snow scene, *c*.1948–50, Edward Le Bas

Chimney pot and window, *c*.1930, George Bergen

In the Forum, Rome, 1935, Vanessa Bell

The harbour, St Tropez, 1921, Vanessa Bell

The trio, *c*.1915, Walter Richard Sickert; sometimes called *Three
 girls in blue*; formerly owned by Duncan Grant; on loan to
 Charleston Trust

Harbour, St Jean de Luz, *c*.1920, Abel Gerbaud

Inside Charleston barn, *c*.1945–50, Vanessa Bell

From an English sporting print, *c*.1912, Frederick Etchells; on loan to
 Charleston Trust

Female figure, *c*.1919, pencil, André Derain

Portrait of Clive Bell, 1908, pencil, Henry Lamb

Head of a woman, *c*.1920, etching, André Derain; dedicated to Clive
 Bell

The captain of the hockey team, *c*.1940, Margaret Thomas

Eleanor, 1951, Roger de Grey

6. Door of Clive Bell's study. Upper panel, *c.* 1917, lower panel, 1958, Duncan Grant

The Dining Room

Sponsored by the late Marguerite Duthuit, her son, Claude, and Pierre Matisse, Paris and New York, in memory of Georges Duthuit

This room was always used as a dining room, although children's lessons were sometimes held here. It must, however, have appeared a more confined space until the exposure, sometime in the mid-1920s, of the large fireplace which had been boarded over. The niche above the arched grate received its present shape from Roger Fry, who worked on it using a hammer and a cold chisel.

A large painting of 1918 by Grant (*Interior*, Ulster Museum, Belfast) shows a sparse, undecorated room containing a sturdy, square table, now in the kitchen, and the figures of Vanessa Bell and David Garnett. The strikingly stencilled walls were executed in the mid-1940s by Vanessa Bell, Duncan Grant, Quentin Bell and Angelica Garnett.

It was in this room that all meals were taken (to which people were summoned – except at breakfast time – by a hand bell on the hall table), although in the summer everyone would often sit outside for tea. Food was brought in from the kitchen through the curtained doorway, wine from the cellar. In later years, few paintings were made showing the interior of the room, though Duncan Grant's of Helen Anrep seated at the table in the evening is still in the house (in Maynard Keynes's room upstairs).

CONTENTS

English piano, inscribed 'Jacobus et Abraham Furchman Londini Fecerunt 1775', inherited by Duncan Grant from his father, Bartle; on the piano, two Spanish jugs and a fruit bowl made by Quentin Bell and decorated by Vanessa Bell, *c.* 1960

English glass cabinet, late nineteenth-century, containing decanters and brandy glasses (from the Stephen family's London home, Hyde Park Gate); on top: Chinese ceramic house tile

7. The dining room. Table top, *c.* 1952, Vanessa Bell

On the window-sill: Staffordshire figures

Provençal cupboard, for crockery, tableware and condiments

Small table for telephone, *c*.1945–50, decorated by Duncan Grant

Venetian side table, eighteenth-century

Hanging curtain of *Clouds* fabric, 1932, spun rayon, designed by Duncan Grant for Allan Walton Ltd; original material

Two Provençal open armchairs with quilted upholstery, early nineteenth-century

On the mantelpiece: Spanish, English and Italian plates; Italian jug†

In fireplace niches: two English flower vases, nineteenth-century, bought in London in 1919 by Duncan Grant,† Staffordshire figure in central niche†

Fireplace decoration, *c*.1945, by Duncan Grant

Circular dining table painted by Vanessa Bell; this came to Charleston in 1934 and had a more elaborate decorated surface until repainted by Vanessa Bell *c*.1952†

Six red lacquer and cane chairs from the Omega Workshops, designed by Roger Fry, 1913†

Ceramic and bead lampshade above the table, by Quentin Bell †

Italian chintz curtains and window seat

PICTURES

The cat ('Opussyquinusque'), *c*.1932, Duncan Grant

Portrait of Lytton Strachey, 1913, Duncan Grant; painted at Asham House, the home of Virginia and Leonard Woolf; bequeathed to the Charleston Trust by Barbara Bagenal to whom it had been left by Clive Bell in 1964

Primula in a vase, *c*.1930, Vanessa Bell, inscribed 'VB to DG'

Flowers, *c*.1911, Roderic O'Conor

Seated female figure, 1922, chalk, Marcel Gimond

Portrait of Saxon Sydney-Turner at the piano, 1908, Vanessa Bell; bequeathed to the Charleston Trust by Barbara Bagenal who had been given it by the artist

8. *The dining room window, Charleston* (Duncan Grant and
   Angelica Bell), *c.* 1940, Vanessa Bell

9. *The kitchen, Charleston*, 1943, Vanessa Bell, now hanging in the upstairs
   landing

By the fire, 1916, Duncan Grant; painted at Wissett Lodge, Suffolk, where Grant and Vanessa Bell (the figure by the fire) were living prior to their move to Charleston; on loan to the Charleston Trust

Hotel garden, Florence, 1909, Vanessa Bell

The Kitchen (Not Open to the Public)
Sponsored by the Robert L. Huffines, Jr Foundation, Richmond, Virginia

The kitchen remains much the same, though differently equipped, as it was when depicted by Vanessa Bell in her 1943 *The kitchen, Charleston* (which now hangs on the end wall of the upstairs landing). The boxed-in staircase leads direct to the attic with its servants' quarters known as High Holborn. Next to it, a door originally led to a wash house and pump room where water was pumped daily before the introduction of more sophisticated plumbing. In 1939, the area was covered in to make a small sitting room for the Higgens family (see introduction) and the wash house was turned into a studio.

CONTENTS

The decorations on the cupboard doors, *c.*1950–55, oil on canvas, are by Vanessa Bell; those on the lower doors (with decorations beneath them, *c.*1918, by Duncan Grant) were presented, after purchase in London, in 1976, by Sally and Richard Morphet, to the Charleston Trust†

Tiles behind the Aga (commemorating Grace Higgens) and the sink, 1985, made and decorated by Quentin Bell

Serving dishes on the mantelshelf, blue and white, from the Stephen family home at Hyde Park Gate, London

Curtain fabric, 1985–6, designed and printed by Cressida Bell

From the kitchen, the visitor passes through a lobby with doors down to the cellar and, out to the left, to the courtyard (at the back of which, on the coal-house roof can be seen the House Leek; planted there by Julian Bell before he went to Spain, it has

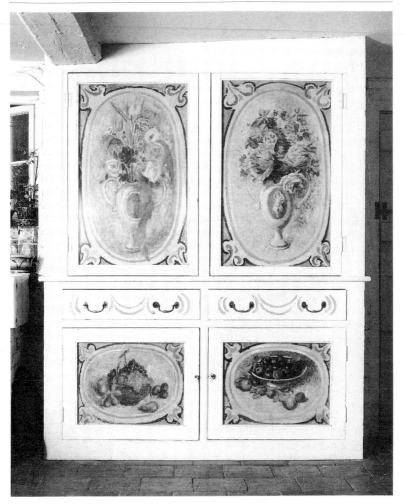

10. Kitchen cupboard, *c.* 1950–55, Vanessa Bell

flourished ever since); the door on the right (now a store cupboard) originally led through to the dairy room (now Vanessa Bell's bedroom). In the front hall of the house, the staircase leads to the first floor of four bedrooms, two bathrooms and the library. Staircase and landing carpet came from Clive Bell's London flat in 1939.

PICTURES
Top of the staircase
Thorpe le Soken, 1929, Quentin Bell

Outside the library
Still life with oriental poppy, c.1950, Angelica Garnett
The carpenter's shop, woolwork, anonymous; originally owned by Clive Bell

Upstairs landing, left side
Auxerre, 1925, ink, Roger Fry
The garden, Saint-Loup-de-Naud, 1940s, lithograph, Pierre-Eugène Clairin, inscribed by Clairin 'pour Mme Bell Souvenir amical'
La Rochelle, water colour, Paul Signac (a reproduction from the 'Living Art' portfolio issued by *The Dial* magazine)

Upstairs landing, right side
Berthe Morisot, 1884, lithograph, second state, Edouard Manet
Two nymphs, c.1925, pastel, Duncan Grant
Mother, dancer and musician, 1959, linocut, Pablo Picasso

Upstairs landing, at the end
The kitchen, Charleston, 1943, Vanessa Bell
1828 Fashions, c.1932, ink and water-colour design for a plate by Vanessa Bell

Outside bathroom and WC
Fruit and flowers, nineteenth-century painting on glass
Beadwork copy, nineteenth-century, of Thorvaldsen's *Night*
cockerel, early nineteenth-century painting on glass

The Library

The early history of this room is somewhat confused, but it was certainly Vanessa Bell's bedroom from *c.*1918 to 1939 when it became Clive Bell's library. The dog and cockerel above and below the window are by Duncan Grant, *c.*1916–17, and the door panels† are of *c.*1917-18, also by Grant. From a still life of his painted in this room in 1918, it appears that the walls were a strong blue, a colour used elsewhere in the house and previously at Wissett Lodge, Suffolk, where the painters had lived earlier in 1916. The surrounds to the decorated door panels appear to have been green. The present scheme of black and red was probably carried out some time in 1918 when the room became Vanessa's bedroom. Originally it incorporated large areas of pale yellow and grey on the walls to the left and right of the door respectively, as one enters. The concept of painting walls in different, plain colours had originally impressed Vanessa Bell in the Surrey home of Charles Furse (1868–1904) who had painted Vanessa's portrait in 1901. In 1939 the room became part of a suite for Clive Bell (with adjoining bathroom and bedroom) and his furniture, books and pictures came here from his London flat at 50 Gordon Square.

CONTENTS

Decorated bookcases,† *c.*1925, by Duncan Grant for Clive Bell's flat at 50 Gordon Square, London; on shelf: Chinese export vase, nineteenth-century

Venetian chairs (from a set of six belonging to Clive Bell), late eighteenth-century, upholstered in fabric *Grapes*, designed by Duncan Grant for Allan Walton Ltd, 1932; reproduction by Laura Ashley, 1987.

Armchair upholstered in fabric *Clouds*, 1932, designed by Duncan Grant for Allan Walton Ltd; reproduction by Laura Ashley, 1987

11. Decorated bookcase in the
library, *c.* 1925, Duncan Grant

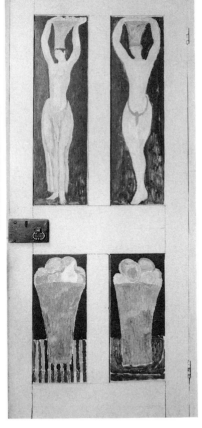

12. Library door, *c.* 1917–18,
Duncan Grant

46

Heads on bookcases by Quentin Bell: *Desmond MacCarthy*, *c*.1942–44; *Olivier Popham*, *c*.1951

PICTURES

Copy of Raphael's *Colonna Madonna* (Museum Dahlem, West Berlin), *c*. 1923, Vanessa Bell
The Jura Mountains, *c*.1910, pastel, Simon Bussy
The entry into Jerusalem, 1912, tempera, Frederick Etchells; exhibited in Paris in 1912 and acquired shortly afterwards by Duncan Grant; contemporary painted frame by the artist

The Green Bathroom

Originally known as the Green Room and used, for some years, as a picture store, this room became Clive Bell's bathroom in 1939. Traces of similar green paint have been found in other rooms in the house and it was obviously used extensively to cover wallpapers and paintwork *c*.1916–18.

CONTENTS

Table and chair, 1930s, by Duncan Grant
Bath panels by Richard Shone, *c*.1969

PICTURES

Flowers, 1959, Vanessa Bell
Apples, *c*.1935–40, Duncan Grant
Flowers in a jug, *c*.1930–35, Keith Baynes

Clive Bell's Bedroom

This room appears to have been used as a studio by Vanessa Bell (her large painting *The tub*, 1917, Tate Gallery, was painted here), as a night nursery for Julian and Quentin Bell and later as Angelica Bell's bedroom. It became Clive's room in 1939. The decorative panel to the left of the door appears in a photograph

47

of the room in 1917 and is probably by Vanessa Bell (with later additions of printed Italian papers) as is the subtle decorative scheme of the rest of the room. The carpet† was originally in 50 Gordon Square.

CONTENTS

Sexagonal three-legged bedside table, probably decorated by Vanessa Bell†

French provincial bed, late eighteenth-century, with head and end boards decorated by Vanessa Bell *c.*1950 for Clive Bell; bequeathed to the Charleston Trust by Barbara Bagenal†

Venetian chair upholstered in fabric *Grapes*, 1932, designed by Duncan Grant for Allan Walton Ltd; reproduction by Laura Ashley, 1987

Corner cupboard brought to Charleston in 1925 and decorated by Duncan Grant

Dutch chair (from a set of six), late eighteenth-century, with wool cross-stitch seat designed by Vanessa Bell, *c.* 1924

Armchair in fabric *White*, designed by Vanessa Bell for the Omega Workshops, 1913; reproduction by Laura Ashley, 1987

PICTURES

Baie de la Reine, Cassis, 1927, Vanessa Bell†

Slops, 1913, Duncan Grant, exhibited 2nd Grafton Group Exhibition, January-March 1914; on loan to the Charleston Trust†

Head of Quentin Bell, *c.*1920, Vanessa Bell†

Venice, 1926, Vanessa Bell; on loan to the Charleston Trust

Two coster women, *c.*1908, Walter Richard Sickert; a present to Vanessa Bell from the artist; on loan to the Charleston Trust from the Government Art Collection

Couple c.1880, *c.*1922, Alice Halicka; inscribed to Clive Bell

Landscape, *c.*1920–22, Othon Friesz; inscribed to Clive Bell 'en toute sympathie' by the artist

Pear and apple, *c.*1920, Othon Friesz

13. Clive Bell's bedroom. Painted bed, *c.* 1950, Vanessa Bell

Fairy pipe, c.1925–28, Pierre Roy

Three fish on a plate, early 1920s, by (?) Edouard Richard (French painter b.1883); Richard was commended by Clive Bell in an article in *Vogue* magazine 1925 for a recent exhibition in Paris

Still life of fruit, c.1922–24, Henri Hayden, inscribed to Clive Bell

46 Gordon Square, c.1909–10, Vanessa Bell; one of the artist's earliest pictures to be exhibited (New English Art Club, 1910, no. 219); on loan to the Charleston Trust

Head of a woman, c.1922, crayon, André Derain

Arcadian scene, c.1909, Duncan Grant; sky repainted by Vanessa Bell; picture owned by Clive Bell

Maynard Keynes's Bedroom
Sponsored by Dr and Mrs Armand Hammer, Los Angeles

When Vanessa Bell and Duncan Grant moved to Charleston in 1916, Maynard Keynes, an intimate friend of both painters, became their most regular guest and a room was set aside for him. It was here, at the end of June 1919, that he began to write his celebrated polemic *The Economic Consequences of the Peace*. He was at Charleston from 20 June to 9 July, and by the end of July had completed nearly three chapters. He returned at the beginning of August and began a daily routine of writing a thousand words so that when he left in early October, he had one last chapter to complete; the book was published in December. Keynes continued to use this room until shortly before his marriage to Lydia Lopokova in 1925 when he took a lease of nearby Tilton House. The room eventually came to be occupied by Quentin Bell from the late 1930s.

The unembellished white walls are an unusual feature although the room now contains three notable pieces of decorated furniture from Duncan Grant's early period. The stained glass panel by

Quentin Bell, *c.*1940, was restored in 1985 and is the only permanent decorative feature.

CONTENTS

Bookcase painted by Quentin Bell, 1970s

'Lilypond' table, 1913–14, designed by Duncan Grant for the Omega Workshops (purchased for the Charleston Trust with aid from the Victoria and Albert Museum Fund, Pamela Diamand and an anonymous donor; a similar table had originally stood in this room)

Linen chest, *c.*1917, by Duncan Grant; decorated on all four sides, with 'Leda and the duck' on the inside of the lid; painted at Charleston

Two moveable decorative panels as firescreen, painted by Duncan Grant, 1930s

Rush-seated 'Sussex settle' with arms, *c.*1850; given to the house by Mary Hutchinson

'Morpheus' bed, *c.*1917, decorated by Duncan Grant for Vanessa Bell (whose initials are on the verso of the head board)†; Morpheus's most famous appearance as the god of sleep who 'sends dreams and visions of human forms' to the sleeper is in Ovid's *Metamorphoses II*

Dutch chair, (from a set of six), late eighteenth-century with wool cross-stitch seats designed by Vanessa Bell, *c.*1924

Armchair, early nineteenth-century

Pottery figures, plates, lampstand and lampshade made by Quentin Bell at various dates after *c.*1939; decorated by him, Vanessa Bell and Janie Bussy; terracotta bust on bookcase by Quentin Bell

PICTURES

The garden, *c.*1938-40, Elizabeth Watson

The Duomo, Lucca, 1949, Vanessa Bell

Brighton pier, *c.*1955, Vanessa Bell

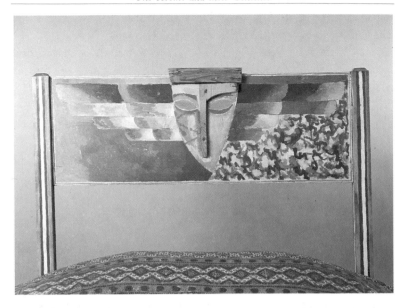

14. and **15**. 'Morpheus' bedhead, front and back, *c.* 1917, Duncan Grant,
in Maynard Keynes's bedroom

Portrait of Adrian Stephen, 1910, Duncan Grant
The barn from the garden, Charleston, 1959, Duncan Grant
*Chattie Salaman, c.*1940, Vanessa Bell; the sitter, an actress friend
 of Angelica Bell's, posed for the Charleston artists for figures
 in the Berwick Church decorations, 1940–42
*Julian Bell reading, c.*1930, Duncan Grant
On corner cupboard: *Still life with Staffordshire figure and wine bottle,
 c.*1940, Duncan Grant
*Helen Anrep in the dining room, Charleston, c.*1945, Duncan Grant

Duncan Grant's Bedroom and Dressing Room
Sponsored by the T.V.S. Trust, London

This room, with its beautiful view east over the pond, and
adjoining dressing room looking towards the farm buildings, had
originally impressed Vanessa Bell as being a possible studio. It
became, however, Duncan Grant's bedroom, and remained so for
over fifty years until, at the end of his life, he moved downstairs.
Vanessa Bell temporarily occupied the room in December 1918
for the birth of her and Duncan Grant's daughter, Angelica. It
was among the earliest rooms in the house to be decorated. The
fireplace was decorated first by Vanessa Bell who then painted
the two doors† to make a harmonious scheme, February 1918.
The green paint which was used abundantly throughout the
house to disguise unsympathetic wallpapers, was detected here
during restoration under the textured white walls, doors and
red skirting-board. The window embrasure,† tiled hearth and
firescreen are all by Vanessa Bell and date *c.* 1925–30.

CONTENTS

Two prie-dieu chairs with beadwork, nineteenth-century, made
 in Dublin and purchased *c.*1918, probably in Brighton
French provincial chest of drawers, early nineteenth-century; on

the top: lead bust of Vanessa Bell, *c*.1920–21, by Marcel Gimond; Italian faience covered vase

French provincial veneered writing desk, nineteenth-century; on the top: japanned cabinet, Victorian, with oriental figures; various family photographs and Duncan Grant's possessions

Curved back chair, eighteenth-century, possibly Dutch or Belgian, with needlework seat, *c*.1925–28, possibly designed by Roger Fry

English seat, Regency period, with needlework cover designed by Vanessa Bell, 1943, and worked by Ethel Grant, Duncan Grant's mother†

Bedside table and lampstand decorated by Duncan Grant, *c*.1930–35;† the lampstand forms a pair with one in the garden room downstairs

Curtains of *Urn* fabric, *c*.1932, designed by Duncan Grant for Allan Walton Ltd; original material†

Chair, nineteenth-century, (?) Dutch, with needlework seat designed by Vanessa Bell *c*.1924

Square music stool, Victorian, with cross-stitch seat designed by Duncan Grant, 1924–5, worked by Ethel Grant, exhibited at Independent Gallery, London, 1925†

By fireplace: small table decorated by Vanessa Bell, *c*.1950

Carpet designed by Duncan Grant, 1925, and worked in cross-stitch by Ethel Grant†

On the window-sill; Benin head (plaster cast from the British Museum)†

Bronze figure of Narcissus, nineteenth-century

On the mantelshelf: two French apothecary's jars, nineteenth-century

PICTURES

Angelica at the piano, *c*.1940, wash drawing, Duncan Grant
Figure, *c*.1925, appliqué, Angelica Bell
Still life with fan, 1920s, Constance Lloyd

16. Window in Duncan Grant's bedroom
17. Barbara Bagenal, taken by herself, in Duncan Grant's bedroom, *c.* 1934

Female figure, 1922, red chalk, Marcel Gimond

Drawing for sculpture, c.1922, Marcel Gimond

The policeman, c.1931, George Bergen

Nerissa in a white shirt, c.1965, Duncan Grant; a portrait painted at Charleston of the artist's granddaughter; the chair can still be seen at Charleston

Study for the frieze 'Bellum' in the Salon du Roi, Palais Bourbon, c.1833–34, pencil, by Eugène Delacroix (1798–1863); this drawing was purchased by J. M. Keynes at the sale of Degas's collection in Paris, 1918, and given to Duncan Grant; it was Grant who alerted Keynes to the *Vente Degas* which led to the purchase by the National Gallery, London, of works by Ingres, Delacroix, Corot, Manet and Gauguin; Keynes himself acquired, among other things, a still life of apples by Cézanne which he brought briefly to Charleston on his way back from Paris. A similar study is in the British Museum.

Cheval ailé, 1894, lithograph, Odilon Redon (1840–1916); probably bought in Paris by Clive Bell, c.1904

Copy, by Roger Fry, of *The healing of the wounded man of Lerida* by the Master of the St Cecilia altarpiece (twenty-sixth scene in the cycle of frescoes, Upper Church, St. Francesco, Assisi); the original was attributed to Buffalmacco at the time this copy was made to be shown in an exhibition of copies at the Omega Workshops, 1917 (cat. no. 13).

Still life with beer bottle, 1913, Vanessa Bell, on loan to the Charleston Trust

Peñiscola, c.1933, George Bergen

Tea things, 1917, Vanessa Bell, formerly owned by Clive Bell; on loan to the Charleston Trust

Lady Strachey, 1921, Vanessa Bell; a portrait of Lady Strachey (*née* Jane Grant, 1840–1928), mother of the ten Strachey children and aunt of Duncan Grant

Copy of Raphael's *St Catherine* (National Gallery, London), c.1922, Vanessa Bell

18. *Arion on a dolphin* table top, *c* 1945, Duncan Grant,
in the artist's dressing room

Dressing Room

CONTENTS

Table with painted top *Arion on a dolphin*, *c*.1945, Duncan Grant†

Curtains of fabric *Maud*, 1913, designed for the Omega Workshops by Vanessa Bell; original material given to the Charleston Trust by the executors of Raymond Mortimer who had purchased the fabric at the closing-down sale of the Omega Workshops in 1919†

PICTURES

Mostly Grant family pictures including Indian views by T. C. Plowden, a pencil drawing, eighteenth-century, of Richard Plowden (1743–1830) and a framed photograph, 1856, of Henrietta, Lady Grant, and her son Bartle, father of Duncan Grant

Bartle Grant, 1909, silverpoint, Duncan Grant; Major Bartle Grant (1860–1924) a professional soldier and amateur cook, botanist, scholar and writer of drawing-room songs; brother of Lady Strachey; the drawing was made to mark the silver wedding of the artist's parents

Chimney pots, *c*.1931, George Bergen

Three silhouette paintings of family relations, Duncan Grant

The Spare Bedroom

This large bedroom, over the kitchen, was briefly used by Vanessa Bell, 1916–17, variously occupied by her children and became a spare room for guests in the late 1930s. It appears not to have been decorated until spring 1936 when Vanessa Bell devised the present scheme in a favourite combination of lavender grey and salmon pink with characteristic stippled pilasters. The window embrasure and door are by Vanessa Bell and the cupboard door and decoration above are by Angelica Bell.

CONTENTS

Firescreen by Vanessa Bell, c.1935

Ceramic painted lampstand by Quentin Bell, decorated by
Duncan Grant, 1950s

Washstand cupboard, c.1935–40, by Duncan Grant†

On the window-sill: glazed terracotta bust of a woman by Quentin
Bell†

French nursing chair, nineteenth-century, from Hyde Park Gate†

English dressing-table and mirror, 1860s, from Hyde Park Gate

English chest of drawers, early eighteenth-century†

Pedestal bookcase decorated by Duncan Grant, 1920s; this was
an early addition to the furniture in the house and did service
for a time in the dining room as a dresser; on the top, two
Spanish vases

PICTURES

The old Hôtel Royal, Dieppe, c.1906–08, etching, Walter Richard
Sickert, the second state of two versions of this subject

Jack ashore, 1923, etching, Walter Richard Sickert; version of a
subject originally drawn and etched in 1912–13; given by
Sickert to Duncan Grant, 1923

Floods near Guildford, 1911, Roger Fry; landscape near Fry's house
'Durbins'

Still life of plums, c.1945, Vanessa Bell

The charlady, June 1943, pencil, Nina Hamnett

On the Arun, 1925, Frederick J. Porter; the river Arun, near
Burpham, Sussex

Mediterranean port (La Ciotat), 1915, Roger Fry; oil sketch on card
for a larger painting in Wakefield City Art Gallery

Still life with plaster head, 1947, Vanessa Bell; the vase and head
are still at Charleston

Still life with Omega cat, 1918, Edward Wolfe; inscribed (verso) 'my
first studies. Edward Wolfe. Painted 1918 in Nina Hamnett's
studio Fitzroy St.' The still life includes an Omega jug and

19. The spare bedroom

book, and a ceramic cat, sold at the Omega Workshops, by
Henri Gaudier-Brzeska

The weaver, 1937, Vanessa Bell; Angelica Bell weaving in the
studio, Charleston; given to the Charleston Trust by Lady
Charlotte Bonham-Carter, 1984†

Still life with strawberries, 1928, George Barne

Portrait of Julian Bell, 1912, Henri Doucet; painted at Asham
House

Still life with pears and everlasting flowers, c.1945, Vanessa Bell

Still life with books, lamp and jug of flowers, 1927, Keith Baynes

White roses, 1921, Keith Baynes

The bridge, Auxerre, 1953, Vanessa Bell

Ground Floor, Hall and Passages

The hall and passages remained undecorated by the artists and
for many years only drawings, prints and reproductions were
hung here. The surprising richness of colour within the five
principal rooms which open off the hall and passages is considerably increased by the uniform plain walls and grey paintwork.

CONTENTS

By the front door: gilt wood carved Italian mirror

Enamel-topped table, nineteenth-century, in the Ming style with
lotus flower surface decoration

God of Earth, wood, Chinese – a late dynasty (with Moroccan
beads)

Two painted Italian rush-seated chairs

Italian mirror, early nineteenth-century, with original glass

By kitchen door: *Female head*, c.1920, plaster, by Marcel Gimond

PICTURES

Woman in a bedroom, chalk and wash, Sylvia Gosse

Landscape, 1940s, crayon, Elliott Seabrooke; given to Duncan
Grant by Mrs Seabrooke, c.1967

Copy of Cézanne's *Mme Cézanne in a shawl*, 1885 (Barnes Foundation, U.S.A.), *c.*1922, water colour, Duncan Grant

Passage to garden room

Beach and sea, 1940s, water colour, Mary Potter

Female nude, *c.*1924, ink, André Dunoyer de Segonzac; inscribed to Clive Bell

Reproductions from the 'Living Art' portfolio published by *The Dial* magazine, 1923, of work by Derain, Picasso and Gaston Lachaise, including Picasso's *The frugal repast*, etching, 1904

Design for 'Macbeth' (the banqueting scene), 1912, water colour, Duncan Grant; Grant designed sets and costumes for a Granville-Barker production of *Macbeth*, a project abandoned in 1913

The Garden Room

Sponsored by The Eugene McDermott Foundation, Dallas, in honour of Irene Martín

This has always been the sitting room of the house with its French windows opening onto the walled garden and its window looking out to the pond and across the fields to Tilton. The room was the setting for more formal entertaining and several memorable events of family life. It was here Lytton Strachey read aloud from the manuscript of his *Eminent Victorians* and where Desmond MacCarthy read and explained T. S. Eliot's *The Waste Land* in 1923 to Clive Bell and Duncan Grant. It was also in this room that Vanessa Bell, one summer afternoon in 1937, told Angelica that Duncan Grant was her father. The room was also the setting for several important portraits including Grant's of Vanessa Bell, *c.*1917 (National Portrait Gallery, London) and his *Girl at the piano*, 1940 (Tate Gallery). Just after the Second World War Vanessa Bell painted a large composition *Evening in the country* showing Clive Bell and Duncan Grant sitting here by lamplight after dinner (Charleston Trust).

Until October 1945, the walls of the room were undecorated save for a repeated pattern at ceiling level on either side of the chimney breast. The present stencilled pattern† was probably designed by Vanessa Bell and carried out by her and Duncan Grant. The overmantel decoration, c.1928, is by Duncan Grant; the two kneeling figures originally held an inset mirror between them, subsequently broken; this was replaced by an oval of yachts and later still by the present basket of flowers.†

CONTENTS

Wool and bead radiator cover, designed 1928, by Humphrey Slater, and made by Vanessa Bell

Tiled shelf by Vanessa Bell; two white Italian lidded jugs, nineteenth-century

French cane chair, late eighteenth-century

English card table, nineteenth-century, with floral marquetry inlay; on top of the table: *Head of Coco*, 1908, plaster, by Pierre-Auguste Renoir, a portrait of the artist's son Claude aged seven; two French vases, nineteenth-century

Curtains and pelmet of *Grapes* fabric, 1931, designed by Duncan Grant for Allan Walton Ltd, original material; these curtains were used in an Ideal Music Room designed by Grant and Vanessa Bell for exhibition at the Alex Reid & Lefevre Gallery, London, 1932–33†

Table with tiled top by Quentin Bell, 1950s

French work table, nineteenth-century, used by Vanessa Bell†

Brick fire grate made by Roger Fry; Italian plate†

On the mantelshelf: French ceramic lion, nineteenth-century, and two Italian pots†

Log box, c.1917, painted with angel dancers and musicians on four sides, by Duncan Grant; one of the earliest decorated objects in the house†

Cross-stitch cushion covers designed by Vanessa Bell, 1932 (left)† and c.1925 (right); worked by Ethel Grant

20. The garden room. Overmantel decoration, *c.* 1928, Duncan Grant
21. Log box, *c.* 1917, Duncan Grant

Three-fold screen with decorations by Duncan Grant, the front, *c*.1934, and the back, *c*.1955; this was formerly in Grant's studio, 8 Fitzroy Street, London

PICTURES

For many years this room contained several important French pictures by Rouault, Matisse, Vlaminck, Gris and Picasso. The house is extremely fortunate to have on loan one of those works, *Le port, c.* 1920, by Henri Matisse; this was owned by Roger Fry, who bequeathed it in 1934 to Vanessa Bell. Of the others, some were sold in later years and Quentin Bell's copy of Picasso's *Pots et citron* of 1908 hangs here now as does Vanessa Bell's copy, (down to its calculated V in the signature,) *c*.1956, of Vlaminck's 1909 *Poissy-le-Pont*. Other pictures in the room include *Portrait of Oliver Strachey*, 1947, by Duncan Grant and *Flowers*, *c*.1925–26, by Matthew Smith; Smith and Duncan Grant exchanged pictures in 1926.

To the left of the fireplace: *Self portrait*, *c*.1958, Vanessa Bell; painted at Charleston and purchased in 1984 from the sale of Lord Clark's collection at Sotheby's, with grants from the National Art-Collections Fund, the Victoria and Albert Museum Fund, the Pilgrim Trust, the Jackman Foundation, Angelica Garnett and the Friends of Charleston

Passage from Garden Room to Studio

On the right

Collage, *c*.1934–35, Quentin Bell

Omega woodcut, 1917, Roger Fry; reproduction

Studies of seated man, Venice, 1926, Duncan Grant

Vision volumes and recession, *c.* 1915, etching, Walter Richard Sickert; the original drawing for this print, *c*.1911, is entitled *Roger Fry lecturing*

English bar, 1920s, engraving, Jean Oberlé; inscribed 'à Clive Bell souvenir de Londres Jean Oberlé 26'

65

Still life, 1919, woodcut, N. Galanis

Reflections, 1975, monotype, Angelica Garnett

Head of a woman, 1930s, crayon, Duncan Grant

Landscape with farm buildings, 1960s, ink and pencil, Angelica Garnett

Landscape with pine trees, woodcut, Pierre-Eugène Clairin; inscribed with the artist's 'meilleurs voeux' for 1969

Angelica aged three, September 1922, pencil and crayon, Duncan Grant

Man in a hat, 1930s, crayon, Duncan Grant

Baigneuses, 1894, lithograph (signed artist's proof), Camille Pissarro

Boats on the Seine, etching, Paul Signac

Female nude from the back, chalk, Aristide Maillol; reproduction

Ultime ballade, 1893, lithograph, Henri de Toulouse-Lautrec

Three figures in a café, 1916, pencil and ink, Nina Hamnett

The Thames, 1859, etching, J. A. M. Whistler

Manchester, 1932, pencil, Winifred Gill (1891–1981) who worked at the Omega Workshops

Mrs Jackson, c.1845–50, pencil, George Frederick Watts; a portrait of Maria Jackson (née Pattle, 1818–92), grandmother of Vanessa Bell

To left of studio door

Clive Bell, c.1919, pencil on paper picnic plate, Augustus John

Quentin Bell, c.1919, pencil on paper picnic plate, Augustus John

Diaghilev and Massine at supper, c.1920, ink, Michel Larionov; inscribed by the Russian artist and designer 'A Duncan Grant son ami Larionov'

Two girls on the floor, 1940s, ink and gouache, Angelica Garnett; the artist's daughters Amaryllis and Henrietta Garnett in the Dovehouse, Hilton Hall

Picnic, July 1921, pencil and water colour, Charles Vildrac; inscribed to Duncan Grant 'en toute humilité'

66

Three figures, Toulon, c.1930, pencil, Duncan Grant
Clive Bell, c.1920, pencil, André Derain; inscribed 'a mon cher Clive Bell/ A. Derain'
Vanessa Bell with Angelica as a baby, 1919, charcoal, Duncan Grant

Vanessa Bell's Bedroom
Sponsored by the Henry Jackman Foundation, Toronto

In the major structural alterations made to Charleston in 1939 this room, formerly a dairy and larder with one small window looking onto the garden, became Vanessa Bell's bedroom, with French windows and double-doors into the studio. The original brick floor was replaced by boards. A bath, usually concealed by a folding screen, was installed in one corner. Vanessa Bell painted several views of the room including *The housemaid*, 1939, and *The artist's desk*, 1945. It was here she died on 7 April 1961.

CONTENTS

Bed, Heal & Son, with bedspread with Turkish embroidery bought in Broussa, 1911
Cupboard decorated by Vanessa Bell, c.1917†
Curtains of *White* fabric, designed by Vanessa Bell for the Omega Workshops, 1913; reproduction by Laura Ashley, 1987
Two Han bronze pots (imitation) on window-sill
French drop-front secretaire, nineteenth-century (Vanessa Bell's desk); on top: bust of Angelica, c.1938, by Quentin Bell
Cupboard decorated by Angelica Bell, late 1930s
Bath panel decoration, c.1945, and *Fountain* decoration, c.1968, both by Duncan Grant
Marble-topped washstand decorated by Vanessa Bell, c.1917
Mirror with wool embroidered frame, designed by Duncan Grant and worked by his aunt Violet McNeil, c.1940
Four-panel screen from the Omega Workshops, 1913, by Duncan Grant; on exhibition at the opening display of the Omega in July that year†

22. Cupboard, *c.* 1917, Vanessa Bell, in the artist's bedroom; the
studio viewed through the door

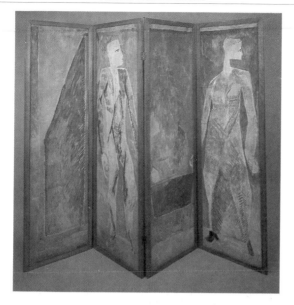

23. and **24.** Screen, front and back, 1913, Duncan Grant; one of the early productions of the Omega Workshops

PICTURES

Lessons in the orchard, 1917, Duncan Grant; the picture shows Julian and Quentin Bell with their nurse Mabel Selwood; on loan to the Charleston Trust

Julian Bell writing, c.1928, Duncan Grant; the chest of drawers shown here is in Duncan Grant's bedroom

Quentin Bell, c.1919, Duncan Grant

Angelica Bell as Ellen Terry, 1935, pastel, Duncan Grant; inscribed 'To V.B. from D.G. 1935'; Angelica Bell dressed for her part in Virginia Woolf's play *Freshwater*†

Charleston pond in winter, 1950, Duncan Grant; inscribed 'DG for VB 1950'

Two oil studies of Julian Bell as a baby, 1908, Vanessa Bell

Portrait of Henrietta, c.1957, Vanessa Bell; the artist's granddaughter, painted at Charleston

The Spanish dancer, 1931, Duncan Grant

Self portrait, c.1910, Duncan Grant; painted at 21 Fitzroy Square, London

The Studio
Sponsored by Lucia Woods Lindley, Evanston, Illinois, and New York

The principal studio of the house was added in the summer of 1925 and covers a former yard and chicken run. Roger Fry advised on the design, drawing up plans and elevations in April that year; builders from Uckfield completed the work by August. The small area with doors leading into the garden was formerly a privy and later a summer house. From 1925 to 1939 both Vanessa Bell and Duncan Grant worked in the studio; during and after the war, Vanessa increasingly used her own new studio at the top of the house and Duncan retained this one. It became his main place of work after the war (during which his London studio at 8 Fitzroy Street was destroyed by fire). After the deaths of Vanessa and Clive Bell it gradually became his living as well as his working room and it was here he would entertain friends and visitors, especially in winter when it was the warmest room in the house.

To start with, areas of pink, grey and green were applied to the walls, the ceiling was white and the doors grey. The black panels either side of the fireplace† and on the far wall appear to have been added at a later date (*c*.1942–45) to judge from internal and (scant) photographic evidence. During recent restoration of the fireplace, an earlier version (*c*.1925) of Duncan Grant's caryatid decoration below the mantelshelf was found, painted directly onto the plaster. The composition is much the same as the one now visible (on hinged wood panels) and looser in treatment and less emphatic in colour. In a photograph of *c*.1930, the earlier version is still visible and the present scheme probably dates from about 1932. The decorations above the mantelshelf are *c*.1925† (also by Grant) and the tiles behind the stove† are by Vanessa Bell, *c*.1925–30.

CONTENTS

Italian chest of drawers, late eighteenth-century, purchased in Rome, 1920, and installed here, 1939; on the chest: tiled tray by Duncan Grant, *c*.1955; painted box by Richard Shone; bust of *Virginia Woolf*, 1931, original plaster, by Stephen Tomlin; ceramic brooches by Quentin Bell

The figure on the mantelshelf is a cast of a sixth-century AD Chinese Bodhisattva, Kuan-Yin, Goddess of Mercy;† the original was once owned by Roger Fry. Two casts were made when Fry sold the sculpture to the Worcester Museum of Fine Arts, Massachusetts, in 1925.

Also on the mantelshelf, various European ceramics and (left of Kuan-Yin) a plate decorated by Edward Le Bas† and a coffee pot by Quentin Bell.

On the floor in front of the pither stove: tiled tray with still life, *c*.1930, by Duncan Grant†

The room's principal piece of furniture is a walnut, glass-fronted cabinet, early nineteenth-century, which once belonged to the novelist W. M. Thackeray (and, by descent, to Vanessa Bell).† It contains glass and ceramics, often used in still lifes by the Charleston artists: Omega pottery; Foley china (jug and cup by D. Grant, teapot and jug by Angelica Bell); Wedgwood plates by D. Grant and V. Bell including 'Queen Mary' plate, 1932, by V. Bell; Chinese export plates and pottery from Spain, Italy and France; eighteenth-century Delft faience plate; small vase by Quentin Bell, decorated by Vanessa Bell; Regency decanters; painted ceramic *Madonna*, *c*.1915, by Vanessa Bell

Either side the mirror: two Italian fairground figures bought near Venice in 1913; an early feature of the decorations at Charleston

Small oak cupboard with, on interior of doors, figures of Adam and Eve, by Duncan Grant, *c*.1913

Gramophone cabinet painted by Angelica Bell, *c*.1936

Painted gramophone cabinet, 1932, by Vanessa Bell; produced for an Ideal Music Room designed by Grant and Bell for exhibition at Alex Reid & Lefevre Gallery, London, 1932–33

Kitchen chair, decorated by Richard Shone, *c*.1970

On the window ledge: various pots, including urn made by Phyllis Keyes and decorated by Vanessa Bell, 1932; urn with figures, 1914, by Duncan Grant; at left: *Duncan Grant*, *c*.1968, clay, modelled by Nerissa Garnett: at right: Graeco-Roman plaster cast head

English silverware cabinet, *c*.1810 (used for drawings and sketch-books)

To left of fireplace: English armchair, *c*.1880†

Small chair-side table, decorated by Vanessa Bell, *c*.1950†

English bentwood chair, 1937, Heal & Son, a present to Vanessa Bell from Virginia Woolf and roundly abused by the painter Sickert when he saw it in Vanessa's London studio in 1938

25. The studio. Decorated fireplace, *c.*1932, Duncan Grant

PICTURES

Above the double doors

Spanish still life, seventeenth-century, anonymous, bought by Duncan Grant in Spain, 1936

Adrian Stephen, 1910, Duncan Grant

The artist's mother (Ethel Grant), 1918, Duncan Grant

Edward Le Bas painting a pot, 1955, Duncan Grant; a plate decorated by Le Bas with an artichoke flower is on the mantelpiece, left of Kuan-Yin

Plaster cast of the ears of Michelangelo's *David*

Three figures, 1912, Jessie Etchells

The pond, Charleston, 1916, Vanessa Bell; possibly her first painting of Charleston

Cross-stitch decorative panel, designed by Duncan Grant, *c.* 1924-26, and worked by Ethel Grant†

Vanessa Bell in red kerchief, *c.*1917, Duncan Grant†

The opera box, *c.*1912, Jessie Etchells†

Over the gate, ink, Charles Keene (1823–91)

Yokels, ink, Charles Keene

Above door to Folly

Design for needlework fender-stool, *c.*1923, gouache, Vanessa Bell

Cat on a cabbage, 1913, gouache, Duncan Grant; a design for cross-stitch chair-seat sold at the Omega Workshops

Below window

Two figures, *c.*1913, Vanessa Bell; recently discovered serving as a shelf in Vanessa Bell's cupboard in the adjoining bedroom

Snake's head, pastel, Simon Bussy

Moth, pastel, Simon Bussy

Jay, pastel, Simon Bussy

Gibbon, *c.*1920, pastel, Simon Bussy

Dorothy Bussy at La Souco, 1954, Vanessa Bell

The Garden

Sponsored, along with the grounds, by the late Lila Acheson Wallace,
co-founder of Reader's Digest, Pleasantville, New York

When Vanessa Bell moved to Charleston, the walled garden was
mainly given over to vegetables and fruit trees. Outside, the
orchard and paddock had become neglected; there were trees on
the far side of the farm pond, grass and small formally planted
bushes on the near side. After the end of the First World War,
the walled garden was replanned with lawn, flowerbeds and paths;
vegetables were grown in the paddock beyond. The evolution of
the garden was a gradual process, going from one extreme when
Vanessa complained in 1917 that there was nothing to look at
save daffodils, to the other in 1945, that one could hardly walk
down the paths for the abundance of plants in the way. The
following year, the last major addition, the mosaic piazza, was
installed, and the next decade saw the full flowering of the garden
under Vanessa Bell's direction. But during the 1970s it became
very overgrown and neglected, although efforts were made to
simplify and thus to lessen the labour: paths and borders were
grassed over, old plants and trees perished, and some were
replaced by hardier varieties. The character of the garden gradually changed – the greatest change perhaps being that wrought
by the melancholy and, alas, inevitable demise of the great elms
which once marched behind the west and northern walls.

Work on the reconstruction of the garden started in August
1984 after the full plan of restoration had been drawn up, and
planting (by Clifton Nurseries) carried on to the spring of 1986,
under the guidance of Sir Peter Shepheard. Although it would
have been impossible to have restored it to a particular moment
in its past, a picture emerged of the garden as it might have
appeared in the 1950s. Of the hundred or more species re-
introduced – including *Dianthus* 'Mrs Sinkins', *Astrantia* Major
and flowering tobacco plant – about thirty, such as *Chrysanthemum*

Maximum, marguerites and red-hot pokers, were the original plants. Of the rest, ample evidence existed in photographs, on film, in people's memories and, of course, in paintings for their presence at one time or another in the spacious flowerbeds to the right and left of the main lawn; although some particularly appropriate new varieties, like tiger-lilies, zinnias and many summer-flowering annuals, were also introduced. The vegetable garden is also being re-cultivated. For many years, soft fruits and vegetables were grown in an area in the paddock, but later a smaller patch beyond the box hedge inside the walled garden came to be used and here were found gooseberries, strawberries, raspberries, globe artichokes, several herbs and the usual seasonal vegetables.

Over the years, the garden will naturally change, some plants will flourish, others may have to be replaced; but it will retain and develop the shape and look of its heyday, establishing its particular relationship with the house – in scale and disposition of colour, as much as in its unique atmosphere of simplicity and profusion.

Within and without the walled garden, there was a gradual accumulation of sculpture and structural features. Those which a visitor sees today are listed below.

FRONT GARDEN

Urns at the gate, 1956, ciment fondu, by Quentin Bell (restored 1985)

Female figure, 1954, ciment fondu, by Quentin Bell (on the far side of the pond)

Levitated figure, c.1973, fibreglass, by Quentin Bell (to left of the pond)

Pomona, 1954, ciment fondu with glazed terracotta apples, by Quentin Bell (at the end of the path leading away from the house)

The spink, c.1930, brick, by Quentin Bell

26. A view of the garden
27. The piazza

Cast of the torso of the *Venus de Milo* (in the orchard)

The remains of *Abstract*, three-part stone sculpture by Caroline Lucas can be found on the far side of the pond a few yards to the left of the levitated figure

GARDEN WALL

Casts of heads made 1986 to replace those imported by Duncan Grant, most of which perished in recent years; one female head, ciment fondu, by Quentin Bell. Other heads will follow to make ten in all.

WALLED GARDEN

Clockwise from the garden door along the house:

Head of Julia Jackson (later Mrs Leslie Stephen), *c.*1863, marble, by Baron Carlo Marochetti (1805–67)

Mosaic and concrete pavement, 1917, by Duncan Grant and Vanessa Bell; the first decorative feature of the garden to be made

Cast after a *Venus* by Giovanni da Bologna

Female bust, 1940s, ciment fondu, by Quentin Bell

The pond in the lawn is edged in tiles copied by Quentin Bell from the original ones (*c.*1930) painted by Vanessa Bell; by the pond, *Male nude*, 1930s, stone, by John Skeaping (1901–80)

The Piazza, concrete with brick inlay and ceramic mosaics, made by Duncan Grant, Vanessa Bell, Angelica Garnett, Quentin Bell and Janie Bussy, 1946; broken household china was used (some of it identifiable as Duncan Grant and Vanessa Bell's designs for Wedgwood and Foley); the semi-circular pool and female head arc by Quentin Bell†

FOLLY GARDEN

Standing male nude, *c.*1968, ciment fondu, by Duncan Grant; this is the artist's only sculpture

28. *The barn from the garden, Charleston,* 1959, Duncan Grant, now hanging in Maynard Keynes's bedroom. Also seen in this painting is the granary, since demolished.

Vanessa Bell's Studio

Sponsored by Viscountess Eccles, New Jersey

A note should be added on Vanessa Bell's attic – or top studio as it was called – which, although not open to the public, formed an integral part of the house from 1939 onwards. It was converted from an attic bedroom with a small storage area next to it; a large, north-facing window over-looking the garden and countryside replaced a smaller one, and it was here that Vanessa Bell painted for much of the time until her death in 1961. Shelves for canvases and works on paper ran along the wall to the left of the window; and a large, gilt-framed mirror against one wall enabled Vanessa Bell to paint several self portraits in the 1950s, including the one now hanging in the garden room.

*Life at Charleston
including Memoirs by
Quentin Bell
Angelica Garnett
Henrietta Garnett
and others*

VIRGINIA WOOLF, *in a letter to Vanessa Bell, 24 September 1916*

Dearest,

It is very exciting to think that you may get Charleston. I hope you will. Leonard says that there are certainly 8 bedrooms, probably more, and very good ones, two big sitting rooms on the ground floor and one small one; and very good large rooms on the first floor. He says the garden could be made lovely – there are fruit trees, and vegetables, and a most charming walk under trees. The only drawbacks seemed to be that there is cold water, and no hot, in the bathroom; not a very nice w.c., and a cesspool in the tennis court. But he thought it almost as nice as Asham. Whatever you may say, I think the country there is superb to live in – I always want to come back again, and one never feels it dull, but then, not being an artist, my feelings are not to be considered ha! ha! – As to the beds etc. – you did once send me a list, which may be in existence. Perhaps Jessie might know. Anyhow you shall have your dues. The green china certainly shall go, as we have enough. But could we arrange to send it by some carrier already bringing things? – they charge so tremendously for carting now. I do envy you, taking a new house – Nothing in the world is so exciting.

VANESSA BELL, *in a letter to Roger Fry, October/November 1916*

It really is so lovely that I must show it to you soon. Its absolutely perfect I think. I wasn't quite so absurd about the house though as I seemed to be later for as one comes to it from the front one sees the least good side of it. It has been refaced with some kind of quite harmless stucco or plaster and has a creeper over it. The other sides are wonderful. I suppose its seventeenth or early eighteenth century (but my word doesn't go for much), anyhow its most lovely, very solid and simple with flat walls in that lovely mixture of brick and flint that they use about here – and perfectly flat windows in the walls and wonderful tiled roofs. The pond is most beautiful with a willow at one side and a stone – or flint – wall edging it all round the garden part and a little lawn sloping down to it. Then there's a small orchard and the walled garden like the Asham one and another lawn or bit of field railed in beyond. Theres a wall of trees – one single line of elms all round two sides which shelters us from west winds. We are just below Firle Beacon – which is the highest point on the downs near and except towards the downs the ground slopes down from the house on all sides. Inside the house the rooms are very large – and a great many. 10 bedrooms I think some enormous. One I shall make into a studio. It is very light and large with an east window but the sun doesn't come in much after quite early in the morning and it has a small room off of it with another window. So we might get interesting interiors I think. The house is really much too large at present of course – but its nice to have space and no doubt it will get filled in time. There's hardly any furniture in it yet. I am going into Lewes today to buy a few necessary things. The Omega dinner service looks most lovely in the dresser. I wish you could come and see it all. It would be such fun to show it to you.

QUENTIN BELL

Charleston Garden: A Memory of Childhood

We were at Wissett Lodge in Suffolk in the summer of 1916. It was generally considered in the family that Wissett was our undoing. Naturally disobedient and mischievous, my brother and I became quite intolerable. It was, of course, Julian who led me into crime; he was older, braver and more inventive. He had perceived that there was an innocent, indeed almost angelic look about me. I could tell lies readily, fluently and with an air of such pretty sincerity that, despite repeated deceptions of the most monstrous and blatant kind, people still found it almost impossible not to believe what I said. Our misdoings at Wissett are important here only because they established our reputations when we arrived at Charleston and helped to make us as happy there as any children can hope to be. Neither Clive nor Vanessa believed in the value of discipline, or were by nature disciplinarians, and Clive was away most of the time anyway. Duncan we did not take seriously. Bunny Garnett sometimes lost his temper with us, but he had no authority over us and sought none. We had a nurse until 1917, thereafter we had a governess; and, if I had been on my own, they could have controlled me. But with Julian to lead me, I learned how to avoid, deceive and outwit them. In the eyes of the grown-ups we had one virtue: we did not need to be amused. We could be trusted to amuse ourselves with games of our own invention. When I was about eleven or twelve I used to bicycle into Lewes (the roads were in those days very safe) and purchase gunpowder from a shop which still had a few customers who used the old muzzle-loaders. The grown-ups must have noticed the occasional explosions which startled the birds in the garden and were sometimes accompanied by fragments of flying metal, but I can remember no enquiry, and certainly no reprimand. All this enabled us to enjoy Charleston to the full, and I am still grateful for the policy of wise neglect which made it for us so happy a place.

We arrived in October 1916. 'We' consisted of my nurse Mabel Selwood and perhaps her sister Flossie (although I think she was got with child by a policeman about this time), perhaps another domestic from London, Vanessa, Duncan and Bunny, us two boys and, I suppose, the dog, Henry.

Vanessa had, of course, made a reconnaissance. After tea at 46 Gordon Square she gave an account of Charleston. Finding a piece of paper and a pencil she described the general shape of the demesne. I remember the extraordinarily slow, sure-handed way in which she used her pencil, drawing the rectangular shapes of the house and the farm buildings and then, making two bold circles, she explained that there was a lake in front of the house and another behind it. The ponds were larger then than they are now but, even so, this was an exaggeration.

It was a family joke that Vanessa always did get things the wrong size, and somewhere in the family newspaper (which flourished at Charleston in the 1920s) there was a clerihew inspired by the fact that she had seen a chicken perched on the window-sill of what is now called Duncan's bedroom and when it flew away observed that it was only a sparrow:

> Vanessa
> Saw a chicken on the dresser
> It turned out to be
> The ghost of a flea.

Her over-estimate caused me no disappointment: at the age of six I can have had only a very imprecise idea of what a lake would be like, and the front pond at Charleston seemed vast. In my imagination it could become an ocean. Nevertheless, there *was* a disappointment. Just before we left London I was taken, for the first time in my life, to the cinema. Believe it or not, they were already making films about Scott of the Antarctic. I remember a great deal of snow and a great many shots of penguins waddling hither and thither. At the time I believed that it had all been made live, even the gallant gentleman walking out into the cold to save his companions. I was immensely enthusiastic about the whole business and got it into my head that in travelling south from London we were making for the Pole – as in a sense we were – and that we were engaged in Antarctic exploration. Driving to Victoria I perceived, or persuaded myself that I perceived, a flurry of snow; but when we arrived at Berwick station and were driven off through damp green fields on what was in fact a rather muggy afternoon, the sight of the Downs, mountains which bore not a flake of snow on them, depressed me enormously.

Some kind person found a comfortable answer. He or she pointed out that there is a part of the Arctic named Greenland which must therefore consist of green fields. I adopted this ingenious idea with enthusiasm. For many days we were Arctic explorers finding and naming the woods and fields around Charleston with a perfectly good conscience.

The countryside was not then so very different from what it is now. The hills were smoother in appearance for they were grazed by sheep, so that it was only on very steep slopes that the even lawn gave way to long, rough grass; there were far fewer fences. The summits provided the most delightful springy surface for walking and there were still a few genuine dew-ponds puddled with clay and straw and not concreted. The big chalk pit near by Bo-Peep cottage had recently been abandoned and great boulders would roll down every winter. Over at Asham they were still ploughing with oxen. I have been told that in America – a farm on the other side of the hill, too far for the itinerant threshing machine to make a journey – they still beat out the grain with a flail, but I never saw this done. There were no buses, few motor-cars and, of course, at Charleston neither the telephone nor electricity. Life was primitive and spartan, particularly in cold weather.

I, who had been so anxious to discover snow and ice, soon forgot my enthusiasm and was not at all grateful when the hard winter of 1916–17 struck us. The snow was thicker and the frost deeper than we were ever to see it again until 1940. One of my early memories is of walking over to Peaklets, the cottage just visible on the further side of the front field. Here a spring still ran. We went over to fill buckets of water for the house. There was one bathroom at Charleston but no hot water. There was a range in the kitchen; in the drawing room and in Clive's downstairs room,* Bunny had constructed good fireplaces from designs by Roger Fry. The fire in the dining room was confined within an ugly steel grate and it warmed the room sufficiently for us children to bathe there in a portable tin bath. Kettles of hot water were brought in from the kitchen range. I can fix the date because I remember Vanessa telling Mabel, our nurse, who dried us with a towel, that there had been another revolution in Russia.

In winter we explored the countryside; indeed, these explorations continued throughout the year. But in the summer when there were no lessons and it was not raining, we had other diversions. Somewhere there is a picture postcard dating from the time when Charleston was a boarding house. It showed the pond and on it a punt filled with boarders, nicely got-up ladies and chaps in boaters. Above them there was an awning. I remember that awning; its yellow silk in the last stages of battered decay, it mouldered somewhere in the orchard. The punt served us well

* now known as the Garden Room and Clive Bell's Study

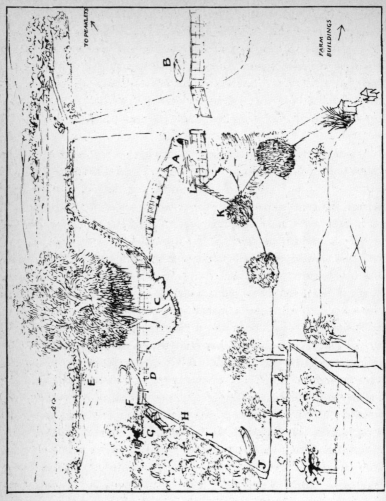

29. The pond, Quentin Bell

for many years; it was the *Argo*, the *Bellerophon*, and whatever else might suit our fancy. But it was when we were playing with toys, the flotillas of tiny craft which we made for ourselves, that the pond could most satisfactorily be enlarged into an open sea.

I have attempted to describe that ocean by means of a drawing which shows the landscape more or less as it might have been seen from the nursery windows at the top of the house looking toward Tilton (just visible in the right-hand corner) and Selmeston, which is out of sight. In the middle distance you will find the letter A: this marks what was, for a child, the most delightful feature of the entire garden – the River. I have damaged a fence to make it more visible.

I have already mentioned Peaklets and its never-failing supply of water (Peaklets is out of my picture beyond the right-hand margin). Water descended to it from a fold in the Downs running through a little shaw which was and, I hope, still is regarded as a sanctuary for birds. At Peaklets cottage the water was retained by a little barrage and was carried across the field in a conduit to collect in a well (B). This well fed both the house and the farm, but it had an overflow which carried the surplus water under the road and into the pond. At the point where it entered the pond it had, in the most delightfully geographical manner, spewed out a great mass of silt through which it found its way deviously in many channels. These were inhabited by a tribe of tiny fresh-water shrimps. A child could see that this was a place which needed harbour-works, moles, canals, highways and fortifications. True, our elaborate works could at any time be obliterated by an insensitive grown-up or by a passing cow or even by a heavy fall of rain, but then there was the fun of rebuilding. The River was always the metropolitan centre from which armadas set forth to establish colonies upon the adjacent territories. Usually their voyage would end at the Cape (C) where there was a great willow tree (also a useful harbour), and a hinterland covered with grass and protected from the outside world by an overgrown fence. The Cape was our *hortus conclusus* and here we could play safe from interference. Continuing northwards one might sail into the Bay (D), which also was geographically interesting, but a little too dank and muddy, even for us.

But that Bay was to be the scene of a childish exploit about which I am rather smug. At this point there must always have been some kind of embankment. You stepped down into the field which lay to the east of the pond and noticed at once that the grass on which you walked was well below water level. Why should not the water be released in a stream through the meadow eventually to end in a great pool by the far hedge (E) where, as anyone could see, there had once been a pond of some kind? What a spectacle it could present and what fun we should have with it. We knew it could be done, and quite easily (indeed, it was by cutting an exit here that the pond was to be emptied in the 1930s).

The trouble was that we were pretty sure that the farmer would be unable to share our point of view. In our experience farmers seldom could. We considered the matter and came to the conclusion that a grown-up must be enticed into the business – not that we thought that we needed his manpower, but we did need his authority: a grown-up would take the blame. We found our catspaw; he was a guest in the house, he was young, charming and very willing to join in our games; his name was Stephen Tomlin, he was known as Tommy, and his head of Virginia stands in the studio at Charleston. We spent a very happy morning with Tommy's help; we cut our channel through the bank and made a water-course extending for some yards. But Tommy was not content with that: he carried the stream into a great curve, bent it round upon itself and then, with the aid of a few planks, made an aqueduct which led the water round and beneath itself and thence down into the field. I can still recall my joy at the sight of this. I can also recall the dread with which I saw the approach of an elderly, dour-faced farm labourer. He didn't look pleased. And when our friend Tommy became aware of him he became altogether a 'Tommy' and not at all an impressive grown-up. What would happen? I half expected the man to trample our works to pieces beneath his great feet. He stopped and looked at Tommy; Tommy smiled back at him. 'Why, sir,' said the man, 'you've got a proper wrigg-me-wroggle there.' He then touched his cap, smiled, and moved on. (I have attempted to depict that remarkable water work; it is close to the letter D.)

Needless to say, our great scheme came to nothing; but we had had our treat and there had been no unpleasantness. It is still a happy memory.

At the point marked F there was a fence running through the pond and this was continued – but you can hardly see this – by a hedge which separated our orchard from the field. Here at F, the coast of the pond changed character; the waters were, and still are, retained by a low flint wall which makes a right-angle turn at J and then, rising to a height of about eighteen inches, fetches a big curve round to K. This regular shape was not as inviting for small craft as the more 'geographical' contours of the other two sides of the pond; nevertheless, the coast between F and J was the scene of some remarkable events. Of these, the most dramatic was the great shipwreck at I. We had visitors, in itself an unusual event, and the boat was full of us, i.e., young Michael MacCarthy, his younger sister, Rachel (later Lady David Cecil), young Dermod MacCarthy, Julian and me. There were some luscious-looking blackberries growing out over the bank; we began to stretch for them; we stretched too far; the punt suddenly filled, and sank.

For some reason Julian and Michael came to the conclusion that we had behaved as English boys should. To me it appeared that first we had screamed, then, finding that the water came barely to our waists, climbed out on to the bank. Would the offspring of another nation have sunk? Or would they, in an irresponsible manner, have swum off in all directions? I could not tell, but for years I cherished the memory of our bull-dog fortitude and perfect *sang froid*.

That straight precipitous coast is indeed connected with another glorious episode. It was here, at G, that my brother and I constructed the defences of Charleston. It showed some tactical insight for our trench – in those days all soldiers had trenches – ran parallel with the margin of the pond and we levelled our wooden rifles across a muddy parapet at the water. Only a foe who was so inconsiderate as to approach us from the flank could discomfort us. This, in fact, was what happened when Duncan, unaware of our earthworks, wandered and fell into the trench. I suppose it wasn't really very deep, and Duncan was assisted by a preserving angel. No harm was done, but on that occasion we were told to call an armistice.

This straight low shore of the pond is also connected with Duncan's gazebo (H), an odd interjection in the history of Charleston Garden. The gazebo began in about 1933 as a portable wattle hut, a thing which sat upon a wooden platform and could be turned to face the sun. In the following year, it made its way into the orchard and there, if I remember rightly, it served as a stage on which my sister, with another girl and Mr Francis Birrell, gave a spirited performance of *Les Précieuses Ridicules*. Then the hut was put upon a platform raised above the waters of the pond. There it stood for some time until it rotted and was blown away in a gale. But the infrastructure remained and upon this Duncan indulged his taste for exotic features (at one time he tried to import flamingoes). He built a hut of timber, hardboard and straw matting. This gazebo was decorated in the Chinese manner; it was adorned with brilliant colours and arresting designs. It looked very fine indeed and it lasted in all its glory for a summer. But the first of the autumn gales brought it down.

Returning to my picture. The flint wall which contained the

pond on its westward shore met the garden wall which faced the road at a point which I have called K, and here there was a holly bush. These walls were extended in the form of a railing, which now stands on dry land but which then ran through the pond leaving a shallow bay on the landward side (K–L). When I first knew Charleston these railings stood in sufficient depth of water for a child to clutch them and let its feet float up behind (it was our first swimming lesson). In the bay we sometimes saw the carp collect in a great shoal and spawn. Later, one would notice multitudes of minute fry, which by high summer would have grown to sardine size and would drift in company for a while, afterwards to disperse. The pond at that time was populated by eels. One saw little of them unless thunder was imminent, when they would bury their heads in the mud and flourish their tails hysterically in the air.

On the shore by the railings the ground rose steeply. I suppose it had been embanked to make the road. From the neighbouring river came riparian settlements together with a variety of earthworks; in the making of these we cut into a vein of blue clay. It could be quarried with a trowel and cut away smooth and clean. It could also be modelled, and it was found that if small quantities were thrown into the nursery fire, they would either explode, which was fun, or turn hard as stone and acquire a lovely salmon pink colour, which was still better. For us the discovery of that protean substance at our very door was momentous.

We have now circumnavigated the pond.

I suppose that one tends to exaggerate the degree to which we were isolated. After all, a postman usually turned up during the course of the morning and in return for innumerable cups of tea would regale the kitchen with all the gossip that he had acquired on his beat; and the postman also brought Vanessa's favourite newspaper, the *Daily Mirror* (it was valued for its illustrations). There were no buses on the roads but you could bicycle to the

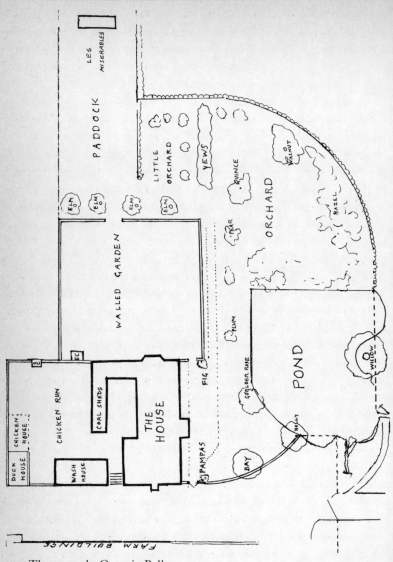

30. The grounds, Quentin Bell

stations at Glynde or at Berwick, where Mr Sutton's taxi could be hired by plutocrats and Happy Jack, the mad milkman, would take the luggage up to Charleston. In fine weather one walked from Berwick, and I remember doing so one very hot morning when Clive was in high good humour, he having been stopped by men who were cutting a field and asked for footing money – sixpence; a survival from the days of human sacrifice noted by Frazer and just the kind of folklore that Clive most appreciated. In the same way, it pleased him that, although our neighbours might cut down, they would never burn an elm, and although they would sometimes kill a hare, it was always for sale – to eat her was impossible: *she* might so easily turn out to be a witch. Beliefs of this kind were still very strong, although most people would have refused to talk about them twenty years later when there were buses to take you to the cinema in Lewes and every family had its radio.

I digress. Let us at this point disregard my picture and consult a rough plan of Charleston as it was before 1925 when the big studio was added behind the house.

Imagine then that we are approaching Charleston with the pond on our right and the farm buildings on our left. At that time, the farm buildings were lovely to look at; there was a fine granary with steps leading up to it which has been demolished, and to that extent Charleston has been permanently impoverished.

The garden gates were set between rectangular pillars surmounted by rather ugly squat pyramids; the urns were a much later addition. The wide gravel path was where it is but the façade of the house was different. The front door was adorned, if that be the word, with a Victorian porch projecting out into the gravel with two ugly narrow windows in its sides and a high pitched roof, the ghost of which is still visible on the wall above. I don't think that that porch was removed until after the Second World War, when a new door was hung, a door which had come from a bombed building in London. Then and for many years all that side of the house and most of the south side was clothed in vivid red Virginia creeper. Hack it down, drag it down, poison its roots, anything – and each year it grew up taller, hardier, and more angrily crimson. We won in the end, and a lovely white clematis took its place, a clematis that was so obviously a stage prop that Janie Bussy used to insist that it was our duty to employ a blonde in a white nightdress with long plaits and a seraphic expression to lean out of what had become my bedroom window.* Perhaps one day the Charleston Trust will arrange for this.

Standing by the porch one could see what was for many years the most respectable part of the garden, the lawn. By the gateway there grew a big clump of pampas grass, a bay bush by the wall, and by the side of the pond a guelder rose. The fig tree by the walled garden gate already grew and was a reasonable size, and nearby there were Victoria plums. There was a very tall pear tree which bore very sweet fruit as round as apples. The orchard was bounded by a hedge. On your left, as you walked away from the house into the orchard, was a dense row of yew trees, to your right a little grove of hazel and behind you, bordering the pond, an untidy accumulation of trees, yews, apple trees, and the bullace plums which I am glad to say still survive in some form. Over on this side – I could mark the spot – Mr Keynes would retire with a book or a newspaper after lunch. There was also the so-called 'safety tree' – a walnut which left the ground at so gentle an angle that one might run straight up into the safety of its less accessible branches. Here also was the quince, which still survives. In the middle was an open space, one of the very few places – in fact, the only place – where a 'proper' game, tennis quoits, was played; for the most part 'proper' games requiring special apparatus and ready-made rules never prospered at Charleston. There were times when the open space became a flourishing bed of stinging nettles. I once ran through it in order to test a theory that if one

* now known as Maynard Keynes's Bedroom

ran fast enough the nettles would not have time to sting. The experiment was not repeated.

Beyond the yew hedge which marked the westward extremity of the orchard proper there was a further barrier hedge, largely composed of bramble, which was continued to form the paddock (which no longer exists). Between these two barriers was the little orchard, in which grew apple trees with small bright red apples which made exceedingly good eating. We called them quarandines. Did we invent that name? It seems improbable. In the northern wall of the walled garden there was a door; parallel and beyond that wall, a row of noble elms. There was also an even finer row of elms, some thirty of them, standing as a wind-break out in the field towards Compton Wood. These elms have gone the way of all elms in our part of the world.

In the very hot summer of 1921 the pond almost dried up; multitudes of carp collected in the deep pool beside the willow tree and also in a pool near the Bay; there were many dead fish rotting upon the intervening mud flats. We took out some of the survivors and put them into other ponds which still kept some water. There was, and still is, a rather nasty muddy pond in the back field and, over by Compton Wood, there used to be a sheep-dip which contained water clear enough and deep enough for bathing. I think we also put some fish into the big pond in front of Tilton. I wonder if any of their descendants survive?

About ten years later our pond was, as I have said, deliberately emptied. A channel was cut just where we and Stephen Tomlin had made our canal. Now it was the turn of the eels to perish; they were stranded upon freezing mud flats. My brother and I shot them with an air gun; the pellet stunned but did not kill them. In my experience you can only kill an eel by cutting off its head. But a stunned eel can be retrieved if you fasten boards to your boots in order to ski across the mud, and can then be put into salt water where it will live for forty-eight hours at the end of which it can be properly killed and, being cleansed by the salt water, will taste excellent. On one occasion we shot what seemed to be an eel but turned out to be a large goldfish; it was not seriously damaged – the pellet had gone through its dorsal fin – and we put it in the new pond that had been made in the walled garden; there it swam about quite happily, or so it seemed, until years later it was caught and eaten by a dog.

I once saw a heron seize and try to swallow an eel by the pond. It managed well enough for about a third of the creature's length, although you could see the bird's long neck convulsed by the struggles of its prey. But then the effort proved too much: out came the eel. The heron picked it up and started again. This happened several times. Eventually, the heron carried the eel to a considerable height, dropped it in the field and again attacked it. Finally they flew out of sight together. It was the most remarkable view I ever had of the local fauna, excluding the deer which I found near Peaklets. This I met at dusk and afterwards had some trouble persuading the family that I had not been to the local hostelry, the Barley Mow. It turned out later that it was a redundant deer. It had belonged to a party of sportsmen based on Seaford who used to hunt it, but were always careful not to harm so expensive a property. The hunt had gone bust and the animal was unemployed. Mr Owen, the farm bailiff, who was mounted, a dismounted labourer, my brother and myself, also pedestrians, tried to chivvy it away to the other side of the hill. It preferred to remain where it was on Mr Stacey's clover, and eluded our attempts with casual ease. I do not know what happened to it.

I had left you down at the bottom of the walled garden beside the little orchard. To the north of you there was a paddock, possibly once a tennis court, then the home of a donkey, the only creature I have ever ridden. For a time at the far end of the paddock there was a long low army hut where V.B. and D.G. worked on the decorations for Maynard's rooms at Cambridge. Above the door someone had painted the words *Les Misérables*. I had always supposed that it must have been made for the French army; perhaps it was. Eventually the paddock became Grace's kitchen garden and hen run. Look the other way and you will find a door leading to the walled garden. This was to become the main centre of horticultural activities, but as a child I was seldom there. When we arrived it was almost entirely given over to vegetables. There were potato beds coming right up to the drawing-room windows. There were apple trees, in particular one big one right in the middle of the garden and this bore apples such as you might find in a child's picture book, yellow and vermilion, round, big and splendid; they tasted of cotton-wool. Against the walls there were pears, peaches, plums. There was also a greengage – no, that was in the orchard somewhere.

There were two outside lavatories; both of them formed part of the chicken run. In 1918 the loo in the walled garden was dismantled (it must have been a chilly sort of place) and it became the summer house. Barbara and Nick Bagenal, much to Vanessa's indignation, had pitched a tent uninvited in the rick-yard on the south side of the farm buildings (where they were nearly killed by a falling tree one windy night). The Bagenals were sent to gather flints from the fields and Barbara also made herself useful by acquiring mosaic tesserae in London. A floor of flints was laid and cemented over and in the middle a mosaic goldfish was laid into the pavement; this remains. It was at this time that my brother and I decided to found a university beside the pond; the colleges were treacle tins on the top of which we made roofs of cement decorated with tesserae: these were much admired by the grown-ups until they discovered where we had been getting our materials.

Grant's Folly was originally the chicken run. The chicken house was made into a pottery in 1939; it abutted on another shed which housed ducks; this became a garage in 1927, I think. The wash house, with its big chimney and great coppers, was separated from the house proper. It was the scene in which I set the most horrifying nightmare of my childhood; later it became my studio. Into its wall I set one of the three stained-glass windows that I have made.

Before leaving the garden I would like to try and say something of its sculpture. Almost everything has gone – the Charlestonians tended to use perishable materials. Edward Wolfe, a young painter from South Africa, made the first heads; he made them of chalk and he painted them; they were set up on the wall and after a few frosts broke up altogether. The same fate befell the large collection of plaster casts which Duncan brought into the garden. There were several immigrations, but the largest contingent came from the Art School in Lewes, which had closed its doors. He bought a great deal: heads which stood upon the garden wall; busts and torsos which were set at the ends of paths; others stood in the orchard, and the largest, the life-size Antinous, wandered from place to place, from the middle of the orchard to the side of the pond near the gazebo and then to the Cape. There was also the Apollo Belvedere, the Hermes of Praxiteles (both heads), a Flora, a head of Niobe, a female torso, (I think the Venus Pudica *sans arms*.) Clive objected that when he walked around his garden it was as though familiar quotations were thrown at him from every direction. Of these casts hardly anything remains. Personally I regret them, I have a weakness for the props of academic art. Also they were fantastic in their decay, the rain pitted their heads and hollowed them out, flowers would grow out of the belly of Venus, a thrush built her nest in Flora's melting hair, for some time the legs of Antinous stood without any body to support. There were also some less friable statues. Somewhere near the sycamore tree a piece of sculpture by Miss Caroline Lucas, one of the two Ladies of Millers who kept the flag of culture flying in Lewes during the war, may with some difficulty be distinguished from the surrounding undergrowth. It is so abstract that it seems itself to be a piece of vegetation. There was a small male torso by Skeaping which stood in the middle of the pond in the walled garden. In the Folly garden was a piece of Greek sculpture; it belonged to Warren, the Lewes antiquary, and was one of the 'duds' which he packed with the more valuable treasures in order to confuse thieves. I think it was just before the war that some sculpture came from 50 Gordon Square: Sir James Stephen, the Secretary for the Colonies, went to Monks House where Leonard peed on his head every night; simultaneously Julia Jackson, later Stephen, by Marochetti, came to Charleston and a pedestal was made for her. It is also necessary to mention various pieces by me. A head made to replace a casualty on the garden wall; a standing figure called *Pomona* – she has a bucketful of glazed terracotta apples on her head and is made of concrete. Also a seated figure, my first effort at life-size sculpture. Local chaps called her the *Spink* and the name has stuck rather better than the brickwork. A concrete figure stands, or rather leans, beside the pond, into which she will eventually fall. She has no name but has been mistaken for a ghost by at least one impressionable guest. Finally, there is a levitating figure also beside the pond and quite near the scene of our shipwreck. She lies parallel to the surface of the pond supported only by her hair.

DAVID GARNETT, in the second volume of his autobiography, *The Flowers of the Forest*, 1955

My first sight of Charleston was from the top of Firle Beacon. I saw a line of elms sheltering barns and stockyards; the top of a tiled roof – the farmhouse beyond. When we had descended we saw it was the centre of slow-moving farm life. There were old Sussex waggons tucked away under the boarded granary, an empty pig-sty, bullock yards, and across the cart track a fine large farmhouse, with an untidy strip of lawn in front of it, and a great plant of pampas grass by the gate. Vanessa's lake had shrunk to a pond in front with a big willow tree leaning over it, on the far side. Pastures sloped away beyond. It was peaceful and, though the footpath to Firle passed between the barns and the house, it was remote and seldom visited. On the north side of the house was a garden with ancient pear-trees and greengages trained against its flint and mortar walls. At the first inspection I could see that it was ideally suited to all of us. The children would find it a paradise and could navigate the pond in an old rotting punt and fall into it.

31. Quentin, Angelica and Julian Bell, *c.* 1920, taken by Vanessa Bell

ANGELICA GARNETT

The Earthly Paradise

Most people would, I imagine, like to look back on their childhood as a time of protected happiness, even if age and wisdom bring insight which both enrich and belie this vision. Under the aegis of Vanessa, Charleston possessed a vitality which has inevitably disappeared, sliding relentlessly into the past. What is left is even for me – or perhaps especially for me – ghostly, a fragile reminder of the life that went on in the house during a period when I, too, was more lively.

Although nothing can bring back that vitality, just as no one can wish themselves back once more in the past, it is possible to establish contact, as though gently polishing the globe of the soothsayers, searching for time gone rather than a glimpse of the future. Looking into the crystal we see a world that was, or tried to be, self-sufficient; an earthly paradise, both comforting and promising, that suggests to us our childhood, something we all have in common. It is this, I believe, which constitutes its special appeal, for in it we can all see something to remind us of our youth. Its preservation is an act of faith in which everyone can share, thus linking past and present together.

At first barely comfortable, Charleston was conceived of by Vanessa as a spiritual refuge from the tougher aspects of the outside world. These may not now seem so sinister, until we remember that it was then 1916, and the inmates were being threatened to fight for a war in which they did not believe. The old order had been swept away, the new could only be guessed at. And even when the future did show its hand, Charleston, after a few years' interval, continued to offer solace and protection: as a retreat combining an enjoyment of life with the act of creation, it must always have been a very special place. No matter how mature or experienced we may be or how much we have eaten of the apple, we can never quite forget the appeal of paradise or how much we owe it, and to find that we can walk through its precincts, even when the birds are flown, is a powerful restorative.

The inspiration of paradise was Vanessa, who at once recognised in the house a natural benignity that would extend and reflect her own. It was not only her gift for decoration that manifested itself, but the equally rare ability to disregard the things that did not matter, to compensate for material poverty with aesthetic riches. It was her clear-sightedness, her genius for going straight to the point, which 'decided' that the order of the day was to be improvisation, holding within itself the seeds of renewal, rather than an ideal of perfection which, by wishing to impress, can only repeat itself.

But paradise was not without its little devils. The tradition that percolated through the ensuing years down to my conventional nursery was that Julian and Quentin manifested a very different attitude to my own. Stories were laughingly handed on, that they had let off an airgun under the dining-room table, alarming Roger Fry; that they had stretched a rope across the road, thus nearly upsetting the postman off his bicycle; and had actually pushed the governess into the ditch. Even if these events did not all take place at Charleston, and if some are apocryphal, they seem to indicate a spirit of rebellion that, to me at all events, suggested a marvellously buoyant capacity to fall from grace without reaping the usual consequences. If Vanessa found this recalcitrance threatening, she laughed it off with characteristic suavity and skill.

It took the hand of God, in the shape of Peace, and the departure of both Bunny and Duncan for the dangers and excitements of London, as well as my illness at the beginning of 1919, to cast a shadow over Vanessa's world. She herself left as soon as possible, feeling that she had experienced one of the worst episodes of her life, only some five years later to recall them, in a letter to her old friend Margery Snowden, as evanescent. A new version of paradise was inaugurated, more possible because the boys, now at school, had no longer any reason to revolt, and all the more necessary as a haven to which she could tempt the willing if elusive Duncan and his friends. Last but not least, it was a manifestation of her own nature, of something in her which remained childlike, full of faith that those she was fond of could not help responding to her affection. She felt that, if Charleston was a paradise on earth, none of us would find a better place to go to.

At the time I was, of course, too young to go anywhere on my own, and I took to paradise as birds take to the air, or ducks to water. Designated an angel, I could discourage devils, and thus confirm the post-war atmosphere of Charleston. It must be remembered that this paradise was an occasional one; had it been permanent it would probably not have survived. The strain on Vanessa, as its inspiration and mainstay, would have been too great. She needed London for the stimulation, the contacts and the revelations it could provide her with, and the sense that there she was not expected to be responsible for everything. Perhaps it was because she was less available there that London seemed to me dark and gloomy, suggestive of Hell. The interludes at Charleston were by contrast clothed in light, in which I could not only fraternise with plants and animals, but dabble in paint.

I was the only one of Vanessa's children to be born at Charleston but, as I was almost immediately carried off to London, I have no memories of the house until after my third birthday, which I spent at St Tropez in the south of France. It was about the same time that I dreamt of both the beach there and of

Vanessa's cupboard at Charleston, painted by her with yellow discs. It is said that cupboards symbolise mothers, and Vanessa's design implied the amplitude and calm of her own nature. It was here that, later on, she kept the scraps of material she hoarded over the years, and it was these shelves that I rifled for dressing-up clothes. Textiles left over from the days of the Omega, a hand-painted, silk jacket bound with peacock blue satin, designed by Duncan for the production of *Pelléas and Mélisande*, a saffron skirt from China, a cramoisy brocade from the Roman rag market, and a considerable collection of those large wool or cotton squares printed with traditional Provençal patterns, lay folded on the shelves, and formed an essential, sensuous element in Vanessa's life.

Thus, from when I first learned to use my eyes, I was not only aware of my parents in the ways all children are aware, but I was surrounded by colours, shapes and textures, which constituted my first language, speaking to me with perfect intelligibility of the two most important people in my life. Indian red, black, prussian blue, lemon yellow and raw umber sang their own songs from wall to wall, qualifying the spaces of grey or white between. Each colour or combination of colour became associated with a different texture or mood. The cotton curtains in Duncan's bedroom, where I then slept, allowed me to suppose, by filtering the light through their faded pink and yellow checks, that every morning would be drenched in sunlight. The thick, chalklike paint on the walls induced a physical response, sometimes compelling me to pick it off in small patches which often revealed a strikingly different colour or pattern underneath; while Vanessa's embroidered curtain in rough wool of a squat-shaped woman washing herself evoked both pleasure and wonder.

Vanessa loved English chintzes, which were in those days a reasonable price. Otherwise she only bought cheap printed cotton from abroad, or ancient pieces of silk or velvet she discovered in some forgotten alley or antique shop, finding them, no matter how faded or threadbare, richly suggestive. She loved the way they hung in soft or crisp folds, and their variety of pattern, sometimes baroque, sometimes geometric. At that time there was no nylon or synthetic material, apart from Courtauld rayon or artificial silk. Occasionally either Vanessa or Duncan might be seduced by such patently shiny, meretricious stuff, and unite them with an exquisite silk or linen, combinations which revealed a highly personal sensibility.

There were periods when, instead of setting up the customary still life, they sat in armchairs and sketched preliminary designs in water colour for a textile commission, perhaps from Allan Walton. At a later stage in the procedure Vanessa would kneel on the floor, ruler in hand, squaring out the design in its final dimensions. This nearly always produced groans of puzzled despair as she struggled with the problems of the repeat, usually in what is called 'half drop', which meant transferring the entire design half its own height further down the paper. The difficulty was to ensure that the design itself was organised so that this device for obtaining a certain variety was not too obvious. Duncan, who was, or pretended to be, incapable of such techniques, frequently asked Vanessa to mark out his own design; she had an unenviable reputation for getting her lines straight.

Three examples of such designs found their way back to Charleston. Vanessa's design called *Urn* was professionally made up into curtains for Duncan's bedroom, and the curtain hanging beside the fireplace in the dining room was pieced together with what was probably a sample of Duncan's *Clouds* design and part of a nineteenth-century quilt from Aix-en-Provence. Vanessa, in making it, hoped to mitigate the effect of cold air blowing in from what was then the back door. The third example was the pair of curtains, in the yellow version of the design *Grapes*, which, having been removed from the exhibition at Reid and Lefevre in 1932 of an Ideal Music Room, happened to fit the east window in the garden room. Apart from a few samples from Allan Walton and some chairs later imported from Clive's London flat, Charleston does not seem to have housed many of Duncan and Vanessa's commercial designs. Some of them may have been on too large a scale for the low rooms at Charleston, but, as far as I remember, they did not appear in Fitzroy Street either: Vanessa was an economical woman, and may have felt she could not afford them.

Recently Nick Ashley, of Laura Ashley, approached the Charleston Trust with the offer of reproducing, as a donation, those fabrics in the house that were either too faded or worn for use, to the exact scale of the originals. He also offered to promote a range of fabrics for commercial purposes, including many of those in the house, to which he has added, among others, the *Queen Mary* design. I was as delighted with this suggestion as Vanessa and Duncan would surely have been. As always, certain problems had to be resolved before we could be sure the project was feasible. The same materials on which to print no longer exist; the differences, however slight, affect both the colour and the *feel* of the textiles but, owing to the care and trouble taken by all those concerned, the results are, to my mind, as close to the original as could possibly be expected. Vanessa would undoubtedly have been fascinated by the procedure, and would certainly not have minded the fact that one or two of the designs had to be slightly scaled down to suit modern techniques. The project is proof of the vitality that still resides in her and Duncan's decorative work.

Printed textiles were not, however, the only kind to enrich Charleston. Apart from a variety of things brought back from Turkey, Greece, France and Italy, there were Duncan and Vanessa's designs worked in wool on canvas in *gros point*, or, as we called it, cross-stitch, by Duncan's mother, Ethel. I well remember her sitting on the terrace or in the studio, massively ensconced in a deck chair, with a kind of hold-all, full of an immense variety of wools, spread out at her feet. The slow rhythm of her stitching, conditioned by the length of wool, echoed the stateliness of her manner, as she gossiped to Duncan about his

32. Virginia Woolf at 52 Tavistock Square, London, 1939, on a settee covered in *Grapes* fabric, with the spaniel Sally. In the background are the fabrics *Grapes* and *West Wind*, both now reproduced by Laura Ashley and available through their *Bloomsbury* collection aunts and cousins, and the problem of maintaining a daily routine that soothed and appeased her requirements of life. From the hands of such an old-fashioned Scottish matron one would have expected to see conventional wreaths of pink roses on a sky-blue background, but no: she was capable of stitching the cock and balls of Arion astride a dolphin, hardly noticing the subject because it had been designed by her son. Thus many delightful pieces saw the light of day, some tolerably realistic, others abstract. Ethel conferred for hours with both Vanessa and Duncan about the colour of wool, and on occasion unpicked rows of meticulously worked canvas, in order to change a contour or add a more subtle shade.

Vanessa's own work was bolder, more spontaneous, but most of it, apart from the rug wool fantasy intended to hide the radiator in the garden room, has unfortunately disappeared. I remember when, stimulated by a craze of my own for patchwork, she took an old, white, cotton bedspread, of the kind one found in every cottage bedroom, applying woollen shapes which she enriched with delicate embroidery in coloured silks, thus converting it into something so original, no conventional interior decorator, house-proud wife or embroideress would have tolerated it for half a minute.

It was fortunate for Charleston that Danielle Bosworth, our conservator of textiles, was so open-minded. I do not know what she felt when she first saw the odd scraps of silk and wool, cross-stitch and embroidery, sun-bleached chintz and faded linen which are all that remain of the textiles of those days, since she had never had the opportunity of examining them in their proper context. But she adopted a humanistic approach and became interested in Vanessa's attitude to textiles; I tried to explain that this had little to do with expertise, and that Vanessa loved materials mainly for their sensuous and decorative qualities, rather than historical or technical reasons. Danielle demonstrated her reaction by the gentle treatment with which, for example, she brought the two cross-stitched cushion covers in the garden room back to life. The same can be said of Ethel's rug on the floor of Duncan's bedroom, and the Walton *Grapes* curtains in the garden room.

For me as a child Charleston was a place full of exciting smells, sights and sounds. The first whiff in the hall, of ripening apples, household soap and straw matting, went to my head, chasing away the memory of greasy London soot. I loved the little piles of settled chalk, the trapped flies, spiders and daddy-longlegs which danced and buzzed a crazy welcome in the unused bedrooms. At the beginning of the holidays it took the house one short night to wake from its torpor: by morning, the servants, whose names – Grace, Louie, Lottie, Nelly – were so typical of their generation, had it singing like the kettle on the hob; without them, Vanessa's creation would have been impossible. Untrained and harum scarum though they were, they provided a sense of continuity and a warm, earthy humour that made up for most shortcomings.

The morning following our arrival, after some bread and butter and a glass of milk, I would go into the garden, also awaiting its visit of recognition, to which it responded less obviously than the house although, as I knew, its need of our presence was equally urgent. Here, there were no railings as at Gordon Square: there were of course boundaries, but, with the exception of the garden wall, they were low, flimsy and imprecise. Certainly, they never gave me the feeling of being a hindrance. If, in early years, I seldom went beyond them, it was because my main needs were fully satisfied within.

Such was the magnetism exercised by Duncan and Vanessa from behind their easels that I never remember playing truant without asking permission, or at least announcing the fact beforehand. In my sociable days, at about the age of nine or ten, I would often walk into Firle, bringing back from the village shop a huge multi-coloured sweet called a gob-stopper, or a paper bag of sticky butter brazils. I would return with my friend Eve Younger along the old carriage-way, past Beanstalk cottage, sometimes cutting past Gage's Folly, sitting on its mound like an illustration from a fairy story, and then skirting the green rushes and cool depths of the sheep dip. Compton Wood, said to be full of man traps, was the only forbidden territory, becoming in my mind a vast area of unknown dimensions, reigned over by the gamekeeper, whose savagery was exposed to view in lines of stoats, weasels and jays hung up to rot, as a warning. In the spring, however, on looking down the rides between the magnificent oaks and their companion saplings, I saw lakes of bluebells flooding the shadows. Elsewhere, there grew mushrooms and cowslips, forming pretexts for other walks towards Tilton, or further afield towards the Downs. In the years before I was allowed total liberty, I sometimes spent an hour wandering round the farm with my nurse Louie, who was having a flirt with the ploughman. Here, there was the promise of a rough lick from a calf's tongue, or the sight of a huge, heavy bull confined to a tiny pen, swinging its horns in a gesture of noble, if resentful, boredom. There were also the pleasures of cornstacks, of haymaking, wagons and horses led by slow and friendly men who appeared to have all the time in the world to pass the time of day.

Deeply refreshing as I found these excursions, I was always glad to return to what I took so for granted, the life of house and garden continuing as before. The orchard, containing the yew tree with my house in its branches, or my nest in the grass; the pond with its fish, the bay tree, which I probably ruined in my squirrel-like urge to turn it into yet another house, formed a world that was indisputably my own, and which, most of the time, I had no wish to leave. But the nucleus of this world, from which all life seemed to emanate, was the walled garden. Facing north, most of the time in the shade, in winter and early spring it could be cold and uninviting; but once warmed by the summer, flaunting its humble but gaudy flowers, tended by old Mr Stevens from Firle, buzzing with bees and wasps creeping in and out of the fallen apples, it came into its own. I had my own games there, the secrets of which I would not give up even to Virginia when she came to tea, but its real charm lay in the protection it offered, both from the north wind and from prying eyes. When I was there I was never out of sight or sound of Vanessa and Duncan, and always conscious, however peripherally, of my own importance to them. The garden was a sanctuary, whose special appeal lay not only in its own modest charm and beauty but also in the presence, stimulating and reassuring, of the beings who ruled over it.

Although the holidays were so long and Charleston seemed to my young eyes so permanent, its true nature was that of a temporary refuge, almost a holiday camp, where the emphasis was on relaxation and freedom from constraint. Every year that we stayed on, however, it became more difficult to leave, and as Vanessa and Duncan were invigorated by the sense of release the house evidently produced in them, every summer witnessed some new development, from a fresh decoration for one of the rooms to a new plant or statue for the garden. Whatever the original idea and whoever was responsible for it, it was exhaustively discussed by both artists, with the result that there is in what remains no discernible sense of friction between their personalities; they appear, as in fact they were, complementary. At the same time, I see in some of the decorations a different attitude. Whereas Duncan seems to have thought of a wall as an opportunity to carry out an idea that happened to interest him at the time, without much thought for its situation, Vanessa never forgot that her decorations were inspired by and intended for a domestic setting. They express with love and affection her sense of Charleston's intimacy and unpretentiousness.

It is difficult to say which colours are most characteristic of Charleston, so various are the combinations and so different the mood they give to each room. It is a surprise to recognise that, as Frances Spalding says in her biography of Vanessa, the colours, though so fresh, are not contrasted with, or painted over white, but, as in Duncan's bedroom, show up against a cool, chalky grey. Duncan and Vanessa were following the example of great colourists such as Piero della Francesca, in tempering their palette with muted shades in order to include as many as possible. It is perhaps the reason why they are, in spite of their multiplicity, so easy to live with. Although certain colours have faded, the effect is gay and light-hearted, hardly even sober. One can imagine that, at the time it was painted, some of the colours must have seemed almost violent; none the less, without being chilly, they are cool colours. Even in the library (formerly Vanessa's bedroom), the contrast of black and venetian red is neither claustrophobic nor heavy. This is partly due to the texture of the powder colours, which seem to float on the surface of the wall. It may seem strange that, in view of Vanessa's preference for the silvery tones of Velasquez or Veronese, Duncan should have chosen red for her bedroom. But, although strong and vibrant, it is not a hot red; it is like the warm varnish on a 'cello which, it is said, enriches the sound. Dark though it is, the library, with its attendant animal presences, suggests a temple or shrine, and is possibly an instinctive allusion to her goddess-like persona. (It is interesting to remember that Duncan probably painted this room after the one she decorated for herself, now known as Duncan's bedroom: its bunches of flowers in Mediterranean pots on the doors seem to me to reflect Vanessa's view of herself at that time, as a giver of life and sustainer of summer pleasures.)

Walking through the house it is natural if not inevitable to go from the dining room to the studio, down the narrow passage which is only inviting when one knows or suspects what awaits one at the end. When I was young I ran down it many times a day and was always struck by the change that occurred as soon as I opened the grey, match-boarded door that led into the high, illuminated spaces of the studio. Here the walls, far from the traditional white, are a sombre manganese, bordered with bluish grey. Of uneven depth, these colours give the room an ambiguity which makes it appear larger than it is. The contours of still life or model are softened, the shadows become suggestive, often mitigated by the rich tones of a Provençal shawl hung over a chair in the background.

In the early days, the studio was bare of all but the necessary paraphernalia. Although it was always set aside for painting, the slow accretion of furniture and studio properties turned it, in later years, into more of a sitting room, and even something of a refuge from the domestic activities which took place in the rest of the house. After breakfast, when the sound of the servants' feet on the stairs and the drone of the vacuum cleaner became too insistent, Vanessa and Duncan retired to this area of peace and calm where problems of a different kind awaited them. Before these could be faced with a clear conscience, they would smoke their first cigarette while reviewing their plans for the day, or doing their amazingly muddled, topsy-turvy accounts, dealing with minute sums such as 2s.3½d. for a bottle of ink, or 10s.6d. for a meal shared with a friend, which meant a long, if not hot, dispute as to who should pay for the extra person.

The accounts settled, Vanessa was able to shrug off the sense of domestic responsibility which clung to her elsewhere, in order to concentrate on her art; but it would be far from the truth to imagine that she was self-conscious and intense about her painting. On the contrary, as soon as I saw her in front of her easel I became aware that she had slipped her moorings and, without my knowing how, had slid into deeper waters. Here, there was no need for intensity; the lightest of gestures, the ever-smiling and beautiful features, the ironic phrase were equal to everything. Although always vulnerable to the idea, even when not explicitly stated, that her painting was limited in its appeal and Charleston a circumscribed area, it was within these precincts that Vanessa was, for the moment, entirely at her ease.

For many years the holidays, that seemingly endless stretch of six weeks that separated the summer from the fresh excitements of autumn and winter, gave Charleston a special flavour, although there were sometimes visits at Easter too. Christmas, however, was the prerogative of Clive's parents, the Bells, at Seend in Wiltshire, which provided us with an instructive contrast. It typified a style of life that, although belonging to a past age, was still believed in by many country dwellers, including, no doubt, some of our unknown Sussex neighbours. Even though it was at Seend that I celebrated my birthday – a birthday that belonged by rights to Charleston – and although I personally enjoyed the life of the manor, to which I had not been born, the atmosphere of Victorian constraint could not have been tolerated for longer than the three or four days we usually spent there. Seend not only had all the comfort Charleston lacked, but there was a sense of money in the background which helped to bolster its anachronistic conventionality. It was, in fact, the anachronisms that I enjoyed, contributing as they did to the Christmas atmosphere, and considerably enriching my fantasy life.

Were it to be preserved today, Seend would certainly be of historical interest, but it did not contain, as Charleston seemed to, the secret of creativity and renewal. It was a forgotten backwater, where the order of the older generation over-ruled all who entered its doors. Its aim was to stick to the *status quo*, not to question it. It appeared to be immensely solid; whereas Charleston, as full of questions as of jokes, seemed suspended above the clouds. One of the reasons for this removed atmosphere was the feeling that we owed nothing to our neighbours, with whom we had little contact; locally, we played no social role, and it was largely this that gave us our sense of freedom. At Seend, and houses like it, the daughters hunted, dined and danced with those who lived nearby, organised flower shows, raffles and teas for church and villagers. The portraits on the walls showed them on horseback and in white muslin, their

faces glowing, hair shining. At Charleston, portraits seemed unconcerned with anything that could be called beauty, or any social
role, depicting saucer-eyed individuals, whose vacant stare
suggested a rapport with outer space.

If ostensibly we were on the side of the angels, there were
certainly a few demons who grinned over our shoulders. For
Charleston was by no means faultless, and certainly did not
suffer from the saccharine quality that many people attribute to
such a place. We laughed at almost everyone, including Seend
(once we were outside its dark and thorny precincts), and our
laughter was not always kind. Our tolerance, largely restricted,
I fear, to ourselves, was allied to a strong instinct for preservation,
which led to discrimination – no doubt unfair, and sometimes
resented. Feeling that we owed nothing to the outside world, we
tended to assume that we could be and remain self-sufficient.

When the telephone eventually arrived in 1939, Vanessa insisted that the number not be in the book, and she would pick
the instrument up with a sigh, handling it at all times with
caution. To everyone except her sister and intimate friends, her
manner was laced with a formality that became frigid when she
heard the voices of those she instinctively counted as strangers.
To enter paradise was not easy, and was best accomplished not
by direct assault but through the intervention of Duncan.

To hear him talk to anyone on the telephone, known or unknown, was a revelation in good manners, apart from which there
was an openness, a readiness to be pleased and, quite simply, a
desire for human intercourse which, while only too natural in
Duncan, created misgivings of all kinds in Vanessa. She listened
with rueful anguish to his side of the conversation, unable to
ascertain when or on what occasion the unseen person was to be
expected. She dreaded having to change her clothes, wash her
paint-spattered hands and brush her hair, feeling herself bound
from long-established habit to alter not only her appearance, but
her whole manner. The hoped-for afternoon's painting, with its

dreamy peace of mind, faded out of sight. Two ladies – or perhaps two gentlemen – were coming to tea.

A glance at one of Vanessa's old diaries or engagement books would reveal enough of such occasions to daunt anyone, making her reactions more, rather than less, sympathetically human. Every week-end throughout the summer the house was filled with visitors; often ten or more chairs were squeezed round the dining-room table, the sides of which, though they did not groan, quite often collapsed on the knees of our guests.

It was not always easy to believe in Vanessa's dislike of entertaining, since she was an excellent, if rather formal, hostess. Drink, supplied by Clive, flowed; food, although simple in style, was succulent and appetising. The whole house, before a meal, smelled deliciously of pork crackling or beef roasting, or one of Grace's inimitable soups.

Quentin's birthday, on 19 August, was always celebrated with a dinner party to which came Maynard and Lydia, Virginia and Leonard, bringing any guests they might have staying with them. On one memorable occasion T. S. Eliot was amazed at the profusion of grouse that appeared on the table. Vanessa herself, no less surprised, admitted to a certain confusion about the word brace, having ordered one for each person. Afterwards in the studio, Duncan did a dance as a Spanish lady, his own body hidden by a flat cut-out of a pink nude with green shadows, whose only concession to propriety was a fan and a black lace mantilla. But the best part of the evening was provided by Eliot himself who, almost recumbent in his low chair, told a long story about a practical joke that failed to amuse. Having invited the Herbert Reads, he felt anxious to improve an atmosphere he feared might be sticky and bought, in the New Oxford Street joke shop, several 'surprises', one of which was some lumps of sugar which, on dissolving, released several small black fish to float on the surface of the tea. Unfortunately, none of his guests took sugar, so Eliot was obliged to take it himself and then to point out to the visitors that there was a fish in his tea. This was received in stony silence, as were all his other tricks: his friends were deeply suspicious and evidently thought him mad, especially when, in a desperate attempt to retrieve matters, he let off some fireworks while saying good-bye on the doorstep. As we listened in the semi-darkness to this story of comic disaster, told in his slow drawl, we were convulsed with laughter and Eliot was revealed to me as someone who, although strange, was human.

If the invited guests were numerous, there were also few days without casual droppers-in, whose behaviour often led Vanessa to assume that they came because they had nothing better to do. Such a state of mind was certainly not ours; having something to do was never a problem. Charleston was a hive of activity where a nice balance was achieved between living together and pursuing our own interests. Our life may now seem paradisial, but as a family we were composed, psychologically, of very different elements, no less prone to friction than anyone else. But it was Vanessa who saved us from the worst results of such differences, by encouraging us to dream, particularly when our dreams concerned artistic creation. She did her best to liberate such impulses, without imposing any view of her own, setting with Duncan an extraordinary example of pleasure in work, which could probably not have been combined with any narrower or more didactic attitude to the younger generation.

Tolerant and understanding though this attitude was, it did not prevent feelings of severe disappointment when something went wrong and the miracle failed to materialise. When I was about ten, at my request Vanessa got Mr Benbow, the carpenter, to make four stout boxes about twenty inches square, without lids. As far as I can recall, my idea had been to fill each one with small figurines, as in a *maquette* for the theatre. But realising such an idea turned out to be far beyond my capacities, just as it was impossible for me to describe to Vanessa and other questioning grown-ups how enchanting such a thing would have been. For years I endured the sight of these well made, indestructible objects, whose *raison d'être* remained a mystery to everybody. Vanessa, however, never reproached me: her understanding of our failures was always equal to our need of it.

Although the effort made by Vanessa to protect us seemed superhuman, it was no more than she herself considered natural. If you were a woman, and had men and therefore children in your life, you strove to give them all they needed, even if art – more precisely her own – was temporarily forced into second place. As long as she felt we benefited, her deepest instincts were satisfied. In some ways, her strength was unassailable; her desire to paint, if put for a time on ice, would not fade and might even accumulate riches. Family interruptions rarely caused more than mock dismay; they were always given due consideration. The concept of family life was very dear, not only to Vanessa but to Clive and, coloured differently, to Duncan also.

Without a woman it could not have existed and for Vanessa it was, perhaps, the most important source of her feeling of validity. Here she was treated as the fountain of all wisdom, and, as such, she could do no wrong. She was herself the source of all knowledge and the measure of all action. This did not mean that on the surface she could not often seem uncertain and even helpless, appealing, not without effect, to those who knew better than she did – an appeal that was by no means unflattering, especially in the light of her natural authority. In relation to the children, her word was law. That it was seldom questioned by the other adults was a guarantee of its common sense, even if it was also evidence that none of the men of the family really envied her the responsibility.

Although Vanessa obviously had her share of self-love, and was in some ways unduly sensitive to the manner in which she was seen by others, she was generosity itself. She not only freed us from unnecessary conventions, but understood many of our impulses. Even when they were incomprehensible – as children's impulses often are – she was able to smile, and her smile converted many situations otherwise possibly poisonous, into ones both she and we could live with. The single occasion on which I remember behaving as a rebellious child was one September evening when I must have been thirteen or fourteen. It was still light, and the grown-ups were in the dining room drinking, smoking and laughing, the curtains undrawn. I and my visitor – whose name and personality remain dreamlike – crept downstairs and out of the front door, to dance bare-footed in our nightgowns in front of the dining-room window. We enjoyed a bare couple of minutes of this delicious expression of independence, before Julian rushed out and, with heavy-handed authority, shooed us upstairs. I was appalled by his taking our antics so seriously, surely venial ones when compared with his own far more disturbing youthful protests. But Vanessa soon came up to my room and soothed me, reconciling me to Julian's violence by saying, with perhaps questionable wisdom, that he did not mean it personally. She seldom applied such balm without a light dressing of malice, the irrepressible irony of a mind that was quick to see the ridiculous, adept at deflating the pretentious with sober common sense.

In spite of her devotion to the family, however – or perhaps because of it – Vanessa knew how to organise her own life as well as ours. When in 1925 she suggested that Marjorie Strachey should spend the summer term at Charleston with her small band of pupils – most of them the children of friends – the advantages were two-fold. On the one hand, Marjorie and the children, including myself, would gain by living together in the country, and on the other the arrangement would free Vanessa for a prolonged visit to Paris. When told of it in the course of a bleak London spring, I was enchanted. Indeed, I was so thrilled that, by the time the school was installed, my excitement had burnt itself out.

The event itself was, of course, quite different from anything I had imagined. In the first place, although I was aware that

Duncan and Vanessa were taking the opportunity to go abroad, I had not foreseen the sense of desolation caused by their departure. When I saw the silhouette of their car receding down the lane I retired to the orchard and wept until I was exhausted. It was my first experience of separation. But I was not one to brood for long, and the presence of my nurse Louie and that of the other children, distracted me. Yet to come, however, was the experience of being taken down a peg or two when I found that I was not, as hostess, the focus of attention, the person who was to reveal and explain the secrets of house and garden as Vanessa herself would have done. She had led me to expect that I would still be able to frequent the walled garden, a privilege not extended to the other children; but Marjorie had unequivocally taken Vanessa's place and soon put an end to such nonsense: the garden was reserved for her alone. I was reduced to the same status as the other children; Charleston was no longer 'mine', but had been invaded.

Once I had accepted this state of things, everything proved as delightful as I had originally hoped. We were nine or ten children, whose parents were all more or less intimate friends and, with the exceptions of Elizabeth Raverat, Christopher Strachey and the two Anreps, who were older than the rest of us, we were too young to worry about things that did not concern us. We slept two or three to a room and shared three or four nurses who fed, bathed and dressed us and generally provided a comforting background. Marjorie occupied the library – then Vanessa's bedroom – as well as the garden room. The studio, at any rate for the first year of her tenure, had not yet been built.

Lessons, which occupied mornings, took place in the downstairs book room – now known as Clive Bell's study – where my cousin Judith Stephen was promoted to the top of the class for her excellence at arithmetic. To me numbers were traumatic, and were hardly made easier by the way in which Marjorie invested them with drama. 'If you have *five* peas in a pod and take away *two, how many* are left?' she would say, with a malicious grin that made me feel she might pop me in the oven if I did not know the answer. Her dishevelled, grey locks and yellow teeth, her double chin and brilliant brown eyes riveted my attention, none of which was left to puzzle over peas. When I could no longer bear the strain I would allow my eyes to wander to the view of the pond beyond the window, where the ducks could be seen standing on their heads in the duck weed. The result of this tendency to dream, as seen in my sums, was deplorable.

Marjorie's greatest gift, as far as we were concerned, was for theatricals. Grace, our cook, once came on her striding up and down in one of the chalk pits – a natural amphitheatre – book in hand, reciting the part of Macbeth to the rabbits and plovers. It was her idea that we should give a performance of *A Midsummer Night's Dream* under the elm trees at the back of the house where, as well as trees, there were great dung heaps several feet high. Undeterred, Marjorie strode around as Theseus, in an exiguous Greek tunic. Vanessa, returned from Paris, painted and stitched bits of book muslin for fairies' wings, and Roger Fry designed an ass's head worn by Helen Anrep's daughter, Anastasia, as Bottom. Elizabeth, our beauty, was Hippolyta, and I was a skinny Peaseblossom. Photographs taken at the time show us grinning inanely in the grass, evidently without much idea of what it was all about, but enjoying ourselves. On another occasion Marjorie staged a small show for parents who had come down to take their children away at the end of term. A screen was put up in the garden room and three or four of us stood behind it dressed as little boys, our heads scarcely showing over the top. We recited a poem, which ended with the disappearance of our heads for which we substituted our hands, garbed with socks and shoes. The watching parents were supposed to think we were standing on our heads. This piece of improvisation seemed to me at the time extraordinarily brilliant.

33. The cast of *A Midsummer Night's Dream*, Charleston, 1925, taken by Barbara Bagenal

As we grew older, Julian, Quentin and I felt the need of other worlds and climates. By the time the cataclysm of the Second World War had receded, Julian was dead, I had married, and Quentin eventually did likewise. But the links which in other lives might have been severed, were, on the contrary, almost fervently maintained. The idea that Charleston itself might disappear, that one day there might be no further reason for its existence, was unthinkable. We continued to need it for subjective reasons, just as we and our children were a life-line for those who lived there – particularly Vanessa. Although the house was not ours, we knew that our landlord, Lord Gage, would never turn us out. This assumption was sufficient security for both Duncan and Vanessa, neither of whom were tempted by the thought of ownership: if she clung to people, Vanessa was unpossessive about property. An excellent tenant, she nevertheless gave the impression that she had arrived by chance and might leave on impulse; and Duncan, later to prove himself an indifferent tenant, would have been happy anywhere providing he could continue to paint. They loved Charleston for its associations with their own love and youth, as well as for itself and what they had made of it. They also saw it as an experiment which would disintegrate with their own disappearance. Neither was ever tempted to 'hand it on', seeing this attitude as a possible halter round the neck of their children.

More than once after Vanessa's death, tentative proposals were put forward in Duncan's presence for the eventual preservation of the house and its contents. If he cared about its future, he knew he would not be there to make the necessary decisions, and although this detachment was, in part, the effect of age, it was also an ingredient of his philosophy: possessions, however greatly loved, should never dominate one's life. Although chary of words on such subjects, he seemed to feel that if places and objects had once been loved – which in his case often meant translated onto canvas – they are possessed for ever. He did not insist on this point of view, but it could be inferred from his sensitivity to places and things, which implied an acceptance of ephemerality and death. It was for this reason that, with natural wisdom, he lived as far as possible in the present. If others could not do the same, that was their own affair.

Until I left England to live in France in March 1984, I had been closely connected with the process of preserving Charleston. By the spring of the following year it was becoming clear that the moment of restoring appearances, as opposed to the reconstruction of the fabric of the house, was imminent. Although I had not been involved in the original decorations, with the exception of those in the spare room, I was familiar with the palette used by Vanessa and Duncan and the way they mixed their colours. It was for this reason that Debo Gage, who had overall responsibility for coordinating the restoration programme, asked me to come back and restore colour to the walls, on all of which, except for those in the studio, the old plaster had been replaced with new.

I returned to England on the evening of 29 March 1985, a year and a week after I had left, and immediately went to see Charleston, which I found in its undressed state, the interiors an immaculate white. The experience was strange since colour and variety of texture had always seemed so necessary, but their disappearance was not so devastating as may be imagined, since the character of the house and the quality of the light remained as seductive as ever. The nudity of the rooms, however, brought home to me the size of the task we had undertaken.

Soon afterwards, I found myself sitting round the table in the Charleston kitchen with other members of the restoration committee as well as the conservators, with the exception of Danielle Bosworth, our textile expert, who was unable to be there. Those present were Pauline Plummer, chief restorer, and Joe Dawes, responsible for decorated surfaces and painted furniture, and woodwork, respectively, together with Phillip Stevens, paper restorer, responsible for screens, drawings, etc., and the decorated walls. In addition there was Sara Lee, in charge of oil paintings.

Our immediate purpose was to define the degree of finish to which we should bring the house, as well as to be sure we understood each other. It had been evident for some time that all those who had known the house when lived in by Duncan and Vanessa, or Duncan alone, had different memories of its appearance. For Richard Shone, who had known Charleston during the last ten years of Duncan's life, my brother Quentin, whose memory was the longest of all, his wife Olivier, and myself, objects, furniture and pictures 'lived' in certain places and for that person that particular arrangement 'was' Charleston – an intense, personal memory which, if someone else suggested that it might be different, seemed threatened with destruction. Splendidly self-controlled though we were, from time to time one could hear notes of suppressed anguish rising to the surface, betraying the intensity of our feelings. Talking to one another produced an effect of stalemate, since no one was prepared to relinquish his or her private vision, while at the same time there was no reason why one should prevail over another. Everyone was justified, especially because Duncan and Vanessa themselves were always changing things. Vanessa had a joke that moving furniture relieved frustration, but although this may have been a part of it, she was also motivated by the impulse to create new spatial relationships, an impulse at once aesthetic and domestic. Each time she did so, the new arrangement carried with it perfect authority, so that those who experienced the results could hardly remember what it had been like before.

Emerging from the question of the disposition of contents was the further one of the extent to which their original freshness and that of the house should be brought back. Richard recalled the fact that when he had first known Charleston in the sixties, Grace Higgens was still housekeeper. She had first come to Bloomsbury from Norfolk in 1920 at the age of sixteen, and stayed for the following fifty years as nurse, cook or housekeeper, in later years doing the gardening, shopping and cleaning as well. Richard reminded us that even if furniture and fabrics were worm-eaten and threadbare, freshness, cleanliness and order emanated from every room. It was an order instilled into Grace by Vanessa who, artist and *soi-disant* bohemian as she was, clung to the desire (more or less hopeless in view of the undisciplined habits of her family) that she should be able to find things where she left them. It is true that Virginia said, 'Vanessa never wants to put on proper clothes again – even a bath seems to distress her', and she was certainly not the kind of woman to spend hours in a hot and scented bathroom, emerging from it in filmy debilitation. The Vanessa I knew washed herself quickly, depending on a scrubbing brush and a cake of Marseilles soap – the same kind she used on her brushes. And, although she was never ordinarily conventional, she felt her home should be similarly maintained. She felt too that to the unexpected as well as to the expected visitor, the rooms should present an atmosphere of untroubled serenity.

Richard's view, full of common sense and historically valid, carried conviction, but it evidently came as a surprise to the restorers. We realised that we had previously been over-emphatic in suggesting that in order to preserve its fragile atmosphere Charleston must not be restored to a condition of glossy newness, and this had left in their minds the impression that the house should look much the same as when they had first seen it – in a state of advanced disrepair, even decay. It was a question of degree, and the mental cobwebs began to clear as we realised that it would be folly to buy manufactured ones to hang from the ceilings, or issue an invitation to the swallows to nest inside the front door.

While we did not want to reproduce damp stains or dirty patches which had accrued with time – and, if accepted, had not been intended by Vanessa and Duncan, neither did we want to put the house back to what could arguably be their own dream of perfection, where such things did not exist at all. Common sense must be our guide, an attribute of which both Duncan and Vanessa had plenty; we must avoid insensitive perfectionism on the one hand and sentimentality on the other. Without making things look impossibly new, the aim should be to refer as often as possible to the aesthetic values that had been in their minds when decorating the house, without denying the fact that time had played its part and contributed its own effect to what we thought of as the quintessential Charleston.

With this in mind, we asked a firm of decorators from Lewes, called Elle, consisting of two young women for whom this work was of an entirely new kind, to restore the patination and effects of day-to-day living on the pristine plaster. Artificial though this at first seemed, without this special treatment, known as distressing, the rooms would have looked shockingly new and over-restored.

It was a relief to feel we had arrived at a common point of view, although it was obvious it would be no straightforward matter to put it into practice. The difficulties lay not so much in the changes of style that occur between 1918 and 1936 or later, as in keeping their harmony; and the thought cannot but occur: who are we to imagine we know the minds of two such spontaneous and instinctive artists? Both Quentin and I, the most intimately connected with the house, and its contents, and former occupants, have our own artistic personalities to hinder us: to hold a brush in hand amounts to an invitation to self-expression rather than the ability, demanded by the art of the restorer, to lose oneself in the personality of another. When the artists are your own parents, such problems are increased.

My own task consisted of mixing the colours for those rooms which were not patterned, with the exception of the dining-room walls, where on one wall the pattern had been stencilled straight onto the plaster, which had perished. We decided, however, to limit this operation to the repainting of the background, waiting to stencil the patterns on top of it, until Phillip Stevens had replaced the paper on the other walls, to which the new stencilling could then be matched.

On Tuesday morning I felt full of confidence, happy to be in action at last. I thought I knew what the colours had been, a subliminal knowledge reinforced by the more objective recollection that Duncan had told me the so-called white on the walls of his bedroom contained both black and burnt sienna. I also remembered that the walls of the spare room, with which I had helped Vanessa, had been painted with red lead mixed with white. Familiar with the procedure, I was ready to go ahead as in the old days, pouring unmeasured colours into buckets, adding size, as we used to say, *con amore*, relying on an inner certainty to guide my eye and produce results that would be indistinguishable from the original.

In 1917 the colours needed were extremely cheap and could be bought locally. Nowadays, few if any hardware stores have heard of such colours. We therefore had to buy them in London, at L. Cornelissen, of Great Queen Street who, rare among artists' suppliers, has a superb stock of raw pigment. White chalk, also specially obtained, was used to give body, to which the pigments were added as required, with an admixture of rabbit's skin glue size to bind them together. Although in the old days these colours had a tendency to rub off, this did not matter to Vanessa and Duncan in comparison with their dry, chalky appearance, reminding them of fresco. As the colour dries, the white chalk seems to float to the top, leaving a powdery look like the bloom on the surface of a plum.

I began with the library, which I could remember when, as Vanessa's bedroom, it had no bookcases. (These didn't arrive until 1939, when they were brought down from Gordon Square.) Here the main part of the walls was black, partitioned off in each corner by bands of venetian red of varying width. I started to experiment with mars black and ivory black. On either side of the window were narrow strips of the original colour and I set to work to mix and match the same. Mars black was too blue, so I mixed a black with ivory; this was too warm. I spent the whole morning trying out various blacks on small pieces of white paper, accelerating the process of drying with a hair dryer, but I could not match the rusty, greenish tone of the original. At the end of the morning my self-confidence was beginning to falter, so, knowing that misapplied effort only leads one still further astray, I turned to Clive's bedroom.

Here I had an easy task to match the yellow ochre of the main walls, although in order to get exactly the same colour I had to add a small quantity of venetian red. I suspected that since 1917 both yellow ochre and ivory black had changed, and, moreover, that they vary according to the place they come from.

More subtle was the question of the lemon yellow beam which runs round parts of Clive's room. The contrast with the yellow ochre had always thrilled me by its originality, and I longed to get it right. Owing to my own oversight, we had no pale cadmium and I tried to compensate for it with medium cadmium mixed with viridian. In a small quantity this looked very like the original, but when applied and allowed to dry merely reminded me of lime mousse. I eventually covered it with a transparent wash of cadmium mixed with size.

The library remained to be dealt with. At Cornelissen's in London the following day I compared a minute sample of the original colour with lamp black. But, although the name was promising, the thing itself was wrong. In the end, I realised that Duncan's black had been painted over a wallpaper covered with minute green leaves, which showed faintly through. I therefore added some yellow, hoping for a greenish tinge; too little made scarcely any difference, while too much produced a black that was not green but sickly. In the end I had to be content with mixing in a fraction of yellow which I put on in two coats and, as it then looked too solid, vigorously scrubbed off again with a yard broom. Having achieved this capacity to destroy my own work, a new mood began to creep over me; I had made a step in the direction of the true restorer.

Nevertheless, I wanted to apply the colours to the walls in the same way as in the past, thickly, so that the brush marks would show and the colour underneath – sometimes of startling contrast – would show through. As powder colours dry two or three shades lighter than when applied, it often took a good deal of nerve to mix them strong enough. It was some time before I could bring myself to shake enough lead red (a new, non-poisonous version of the old red lead, which in powder form bears no relation to its seductive forerunner) into the undercoat for Vanessa's bedroom. On the wall it looked like cooked lobster, though it later paled to salmon, a colour for which Nessa had a weakness but which personally I have never liked – a possible reason for my finding it so difficult to deal with. A further problem was that, though

Vicki Walton (the Hon. Curator at Charleston) and I used the same brushes, the marks left by me were different from hers, and neither was the same as Vanessa's and Duncan's. Although their brushes may have been a different shape, we each had different nervous systems and moved to a different rhythm.

I could not but ask myself not only what was I trying to do, but what ought I to be doing? In spite of my 'knowledge' of each colour, I had compromised in almost every case, admittedly sometimes for reasons outside my control. In my disillusionment I was reduced to saying that it was a question of sensitivity – surely the last-ditch defence of the restorer, or artist, who does not know what he wants. Sensitivity is essential, though equally necessary is the strength of mind to stick to what you 'know' is right; sensitivity has to be used, not to excuse clumsiness, but to discriminate between what is 'wrong' and what is 'right' – just as in painting a picture, one's inner eye must be fixed on a definite end in view, whether or not that end was originally conceived by someone else. This was the only way to justify the illusion we were trying to create. As I worked, I realised, moreover, that, in spite of the intensity of feeling that lies behind it, memory is fragile, unreliable and elusive, hating above all to be pinned down and brought out into the open, for fear that it will be for ever proved a lie.

I was perhaps complicating a fundamentally simple process, which nevertheless illuminated the difference between colour matching (something I now feel should be included in all artists' training) and the process demonstrated by Duncan and Vanessa whenever they dipped a brush in paint. I well remember Vanessa's slow, sensuous stroke and Duncan's delicacy. To watch them painting a canvas or wall was rather like watching a sleep-walker. Colour sprang from palette to painted surface guided, it seemed, by instinct alone, and was seldom wrong. Until the following day, when they applied their minds to what they had done, the process was certainly not one of conscious thought.

When I went into the studio I found Pauline's assistants at work on the two walls where the plaster had not been removed and most of the old paint remained. In some places, the colour had rubbed off and others showed traces of rain where the roof had leaked. On one wall a worm or fungus had eaten into the plaster leaving a circular pattern behind it. While the characteristic variations of colour were allowed to remain, these places were being delicately restored to their former homogeneity.

Pauline herself was concentrating on the preservation of Duncan's decoration over the mantelpiece – now very fragile – while also repainting the west wall where the plaster had been replaced. The problem here was to marry the new colour up to that on the adjacent wall, where the old colour remained. Although difficult to do, there was at least a decent expanse to take as a model. Duncan and Vanessa had painted directly onto the pinkish plaster with a rather thin paint which showed every brush mark. Whereas I, in Pauline's place, would have used large brushes, hoping for a result indistinguishable from the original, Pauline was applying the paint with tiny brushes, as well as using sprays and other sophisticated devices. I realised that nothing could be more different than our two attitudes, mine crude and happy-go-lucky, Pauline's careful, knowledgeable, experimental and analytical. A combination of the two was what we needed.

The removal of the pictures from the studio walls revealed patches of bare plaster, and it was amusing to realise that Duncan and Vanessa had hung them first and afterwards painted round them. There had been no question of doing anything so time-consuming as taking them down and re-hanging them. (This was also true of the mirror which was bequeathed by Duncan to Clarissa Roche. When she took it away, I was living in the house, and was so shocked by the bare oval shape that I painted it over with the only colour I had – not quite the same as the rest of the wall.) Pauline and I discussed whether this should be imitated.

I could not help thinking that Duncan and Vanessa would have been amazed at our pedantry.

My daughter Nerissa told me that long ago, when she was living in France, she painted a picture of the family at Charleston sitting round the dining-room table. Unable to remember the wallpaper, she wrote to Duncan to ask him to send her a diagram. He responded with a pattern that, though deceptively like, was not the same. He had not bothered to go into the dining room and look at the walls.

It is hard to guess his and Vanessa's attitude to the restoration of the house. There is paradox in the fact that our procedures, radically different from theirs, are necessary in order to prevent – as far as we can – their spirit from flying out of the window. Had Duncan and Vanessa decided that Charleston needed refurbishing, a word they might have used, they would never have started imitating their own work, though neither would they have destroyed it. Wherever possible they would have given things a new look, and who knows but they would have been delighted with emulsion, with paint that won't drip and even with sprays and rollers – although they would almost certainly have used them in an unorthodox way; but this is the point at which we are forced to part company with them. In their serene evening mood, I think both Duncan and Vanessa – give or take some amusement at our problems and at our way of dealing with them – would have been secretly pleased that we care so much.

DUNCAN GRANT, *in a letter to Vanessa Bell, October 1916*

I am sitting just before having some of this herring you ordered us and among all the fascinating things that arrived this evening from Lewes. The carrier made a pile of them outside the door. They have already made the kitchen a place of beauty. There is a most superb crock, brown with a red top, shining tin tin, and emerald green lampshades. Talking of crocks you measured the lamp wrong and the lamp glasses won't fit. It doesn't matter as there is no oil, but I merely put it in. I like Mrs Churchill, she is friendly and easy to get on with and much more punctual than Ethel could be without you – I really think it will be a very good arrangement having her. Did you know that Henry *bit* that painter's leg? He took a violent dislike to him and I had great difficulty in keeping him back from another attack today . . . Did you see the garden room before you left? It is lovely.

CLIVE BELL, *in a letter to Vanessa Bell, Winter 1916, following a visit to Charleston with Mary Hutchinson*

What fun it was at Charleston and how charming you all were! We enjoyed every minute of it including our exquisite walk across the frost-bound park . . . There was only one thing I didn't like at Charleston: need you do so much house-work? Because the bloody government has made slaves of Duncan and Bunny, need it make one of you? And why don't you paint more?

JOHN MAYNARD KEYNES, *in a letter to Mrs Keynes, 6 August 1919*

Here my breakfast comes at 8 and my book occupies me until lunch, before which I am not seen in the public rooms. After lunch *The Times* and after *The Times* gardening until tea time. After tea my correspondence. All very regular. I have bought my own servants down here, as the total party is large, and Gordon Square is shut up.

34. David Garnett and Maynard Keynes, Charleston, 1919, taken by Vanessa Bell

LYTTON STRACHEY, *in a letter to Carrington, 4 September 1920*

Typically, Maynard has insisted on . . . you'd never guess what: altering the time! So that the clocks are one hour in advance even of summer time, with curious consequences. For one thing Jessie disapproves, won't have it, and has let the kitchen clock run down so that the servants have *no* time. Then Clive is fitful on the subject, and insists upon always referring to the normal time; and altogether the confusion is extraordinary. How mad they all are! Maynard, though he sees what a rumpus it causes, persists. Vanessa is too feeble to put him down, and Clive is too tetchy to grin and bear it. The result is extremely Tchekhofesque. But luckily the atmosphere is entirely comic, instead of being fundamentally tragic as in Tchekhof. Everyone laughs and screams and passes on.

ROGER FRY, *in letters to Helen Anrep*
18 April 1925

Unless Alderney has a very different climate from this or unless it's central heated you must be frozen. Here we sit and shiver except when Vanessa and I are forced to go out into the back yard and try to measure the area of her projected studio with a broken tape measure, which is all that the place affords. However, bit by bit we are conceiving a grand scheme and I've at last finished the plans, elevations and details. It's really the humblest architectural effort you can imagine, for the great object is to have as much room and spend as little money as possible. That, of course, appeals to my avaricious nature, which is almost as much gratified by saving other people's money as my own. Anyhow it's great fun trying to make use of all the queer shapes of wall that these sheds and outhouses provide and drawing them together into a single building. We're also going to use the old tiles – so that what with old tiles and old flint walls, even though there's no architectural 'features', it may make a quite decent sort of barn and if we can keep the builder from putting in knick-knacks and mouldings, why it may be respectable and God knows, it ought to be cheap . . .

This is the most peaceful domestic existence conceivable; there's only Clive, Vanessa and the children. It might be held up as a model of what family life ought to be. The extraordinary thing is that the two boys amuse themselves wildly with almost nothing particular to do. Quentin is always happy where there's mud and water. They spend the whole evening concocting the News Bulletin which appears at breakfast the next morning generally typewritten. It contains a fantastic version of the daily events, generally very much to Vanessa's discredit – a good many satirical and comic poems illustrated by Quentin, and a weather prophecy.

2 August 1925

A very typical Charleston day – incredibly domestic and idyllic as usual here – spent by the whole family (D., V. and the two boys – I wish Angelica were here too) pottering round the pond. Last night we were lamenting the perfectly even green carpet of duckweed which covered the whole surface of the water, so this morning I began to attempt a remedy. I got a heavy rake, nailed bits of wood across the teeth and began to haul up the weed. It was fascinating but slow and also my wretched back soon gave out. Then V. took a hand, but even she soon abandoned it. Then she thought of a net; I suggested a hammock. We found an old one, fixed sticks at either end and cords at the four corners and tried to haul in nets full – but the meshes were big and the weed escaped. But we saw from that that the way would be to drag something across the surface and at once got one of the workmen's ladders and with cords at either end launched it out and pulled it in shore. Some success and then Vanessa had the brilliant idea of tying so many ladders end to end as to stretch almost across

35. *Top:* Angelica Bell, Clive Bell, Stephen Tomlin and Lytton Strachey in the walled garden at Charleston, *c.* 1925, taken by Vanessa Bell

36. *Bottom:* Roger Fry, Desmond MacCarthy and Clive Bell, Charleston, *c.* 1925, taken by Vanessa Bell

the pond – fearful difficulties of working cords over the bushes etc. but by this time the boys (who had hitherto maintained an attitude of sceptical contempt loudly and freely expressed from where they were lying kicking their heels) became interested and fortunately Quentin fell in accidentally, whereupon there seemed no reason why he shouldn't be used to push the ladders wading. Gradually both boys became naked and under our directions pushed the barrage right across the pond and hauled out the weed by the armful at the side. It led to a great deal of unnecessary swimming in about two feet of muddy water but this only increased the satisfaction and mess and by dinner time the pond was practically clear, the trees and hills all neatly reflected and the banks a mass of smelly and clammy weed, and everyone felt exceedingly virtuous and happy and Vanessa and I very proud of our determination to carry out somehow the great and apparently impossible design at which everyone else, including D., had mocked. The ducks who were bought in the hope that they would eat the weed had maintained an attitude of helpless indifference to the vast green feast spread for them, but when they saw it nearly cleared they began to think it a rare and delicious delicacy and can be trusted, we think, to clear up what is left. Driving the ducks into their shed behind the kitchen is also a difficult, exciting and important operation which requires the presence of the whole family to discourage them from taking all the wrong turnings . . .

QUENTIN BELL, *in his biography of Virginia Woolf*

That summer [1927] Virginia acquired a motor-car and a lover . . . The motor-car was considered a great luxury . . . The whole Sussex countryside, with its castles, seashores and great houses, suddenly became accessible; so too of course was Charleston and the Keynes's new home at Tilton. The social possibilities of the automobile were such that Vanessa, much to

Virginia's amusement, placed a large notice on the gate leading to Charleston drive, bearing the word OUT.

FRANCES PARTRIDGE, *from a paper given at a Charleston Symposium at the Victoria and Albert Museum, London, 1983*

Charleston values quickly made themselves felt. Beauty, of course, and many sensuous pleasures – good cooking, wine at most meals, home-made jams and bread: all these ranked high, even if comfort in the strictest did not. In winter you might suffer severely from the cold, and at the time of my first visit there in the mid-twenties was only one bathroom containing a narrow bath short of enamel and giving out a hollow tinny sound, whose pipes dripped gently but steadily, in spite of being wrapped in yellowing newspapers. Yet hot baths were there for everyone who wanted them, and brass cans were brought to all the bedrooms.

Some of those who descended to the dining room for breakfast seemed to have got rather quickly into their clothes it must be said, and the expressions on their faces showed their preoccupation with their plans for the day to come, as they helped themselves to the strong rich-smelling coffee keeping warm in a handsome pottery jug on the hob. Julian and Quentin – large and somewhat rumbustious young men – would be earnestly stoking up at the large round, painted table, while Angelica flirted around, an enchanting ten-year-old with enormous grey eyes. I was astonished by Duncan's look of youth, crumpled rose-leaf complexion and forget-me-not eyes; his thick black hair with no hint of grey was a good advertisement for lack of brushing.

Vanessa's awesomely noble resemblance to a Greek statue of the archaic period contrasted with her dry sense of humour. Preoccupied they might be but this family weren't at all like the traditional English breakfast group hiding sullenly behind their newspapers. For one thing they took a lively and amused interest in each others' characteristic remarks. Anything might crop up, bursts of laughter explode, or letters be read aloud.

'I'm afraid I can't *read* this,' says Duncan, in soft hesitant tones accompanied by much thinking; 'it seems to have been written in what they call – er – *vanishing* ink.' Vanessa (sepulchrally), 'A pity *all* letters weren't written in that.'

I was rather alarmed at first – I wasn't socially confident – but I soon began to find out what fun it all was. A great deal was usually going on: a performance of a play, for instance, by Angelica and her schoolfriends wearing dresses designed and made by Duncan and Vanessa. She was musical and I sometimes accompanied her when she played the violin or sang, and nothing could have been more flattering than finding myself referred to in one of her poems in the house magazine as, 'And then there's Miss Marshall – To whom we are partial.'

Now, as I look back more than fifty years at Charleston in its heyday I see it as an enchanted place – a place of such potent individuality that whenever I stayed there I came away grateful to it, as it were, for giving me so much pleasure, so many rich and various visual sensations, such *talk*, such an awareness that lives were being intensely and purposefully led there – for being *itself* in fact, just as one feels grateful to a very pretty girl for ravishing one's eyes. I tend to picture it at noon on a summer's day, with the tall flowers motionless in the hot still air, their corollas buzzing with bees; a dragon-fly or two skimming over the duckweed-covered pond; and a small group sitting outside the drawing-room French windows in those indestructible and inelegant chairs known as roorkhees, that everyone seemed to have inherited from an Anglo-Indian uncle – talking and laughing. The house gave the impression of having developed spontaneously, like some vigorous vegetable growth, in spite of the display of human creative energy that covered the walls of all its rooms; for Duncan and Vanessa couldn't see an empty flat space without wanting to cover it with flowers and nudes, with vases

37. Duncan Grant, Frances Partridge and Raymond Mortimer,
Charleston, 1928, taken by Vanessa Bell

and swirls (probably surrounded by croquet hoops) all in the
warm richness of their favoured colours – blue, russet, gamboge.

To my delight my summer visits became annual events, but I
have also seen and adored Charleston in grimmer seasons – never
I think under snow, but with the tall trees standing like bare
skeletons against the majestic height of the Downs and the short
grey-green turf of their flanks.

NICHOLAS HENDERSON, *Children at Charleston, from the Charleston Newsletter, no. 2, 1982*

It did not occur to us, a dozen or so very young boys and girls, who for the rest of the year were being taught the three Rs by Marjorie Strachey in Gordon Square, to wonder why in summer we were transported with blackboard and exercise books to Charleston. I suppose it may have been thought healthier for us. Perhaps Marjorie Strachey pined for the country. I can hardly believe that the grown-ups at Charleston, Vanessa Bell, (Clive at week-ends, bringing gusts of laughter) and Duncan Grant, or their regular visitors, the Woolfs, from nearby and, less frequently though closer in distance if not affection, the Keyneses, were eager for this annual visitation, because Bloomsbury were not devotees of small children any more than they were of dogs.

It may have been this slight aloofness that made these grown-ups so interesting to us. We were very much aware of them, as they went purposefully about their daily tasks of painting and exchanging ideas, pursuits that did not require any attention to us.

Young as we were we could not, of course, judge whether or in what way they were different from other people, but those who looked after us, members of the Selwood family – a name that should feature in any incunabula of Bloomsbury – always spoke of them with matter-of-fact respect and never with surprise; and indeed why should they have done otherwise, for life was orderly and quiet at Charleston – a world of peace within itself. The Selwoods appeared to take for granted, as we did at the time, unaware that it was particular to Charleston, Vanessa's and Duncan's practice of decorating everything in the house – tables, bookcases, chimney pieces, chairs – with their own designs, though this feature of the house is highly vivid in retrospect.

Marjorie would conduct her lessons in the morning, and she was an operatic conductor, sparing nothing on the effort: didactic, dogmatic, enthusiastic, she was a born teacher. After lunch there would be drawing and painting with Vanessa. She was unassertive in manner and unimpetuous in movement. I do not think she expected much of us, except to sit for her, although Angelica already showed talent.

For me she also showed other qualities. We were, to use the Charleston jargon, 'sticky friends', and we spent a lot of time seated inseparably on the top of one or other of the horizontal trees that stood in a row beyond the walled garden. When I visited Charleston many years later, I could not find a trace of those trees; and I expect they were really much smaller than they appeared to us at the time. Like any secret hiding place of childhood, they still look large in memory.

So does the pond opposite the front of the house, a farmyard pond, with a field on one side. Duncan has put it into his paintings; it is imprinted on my mind's eye because of its association with danger and drama. One day a cow wandered into the pond and became stuck in the mud. With great difficulty and much shouting the farmhands got her out; but we were constantly afraid that it was going to happen again and we were warned of the danger we would be in if we fell into the pond.

These are the memories I have of the summer school at Charleston over half a century ago: of country life, of the tree-tops, of one sticky friend and of the grown-ups, absorbed in their lives, applying colour to all things, unconcerned by the world outside, inattentive to us, but even more alluring for all that.

VIRGINIA WOOLF, *in her Diary, 1 April 1930*

Nessa is at Charleston. They will have the windows open; perhaps even sit by the pond. She will think This is what I have made by years of unknown work – my sons, my daughter. She will be perfectly content (as I suppose) Quentin fetching bottles; Clive immensely good tempered. They will think of London with dislike . . .

JULIAN BELL, *in letters to Vanessa Bell*
from Wuhan University, Hankow, China

23 October 1935

I have my moments of frightful loneliness, when I want the peace and security of Charleston and all of you frightfully. In a way it's like my crisis two years ago: the uprooting, newness, isolation. But its mitigated by a greater self-confidence, by the insensibility of illness (so that I've got into a routine foundation almost without effort) and by the close, perpetual contact with the Chengs. Besides, I'm beginning to know that all human life is really uprooted, and Charleston and you are exceptions. Most of them live only by insensibility.

8 November 1935
There was a most Charlestonian scene as I walked this evening – a bull water-buffalo gone wild, with half a dozen dogs chasing, and vague people whacking, halloing. Round and about – graves, field, path, crushing a peach orchard and wire fence – how I longed to join in.

VANESSA BELL, *in letters to Julian Bell*
4 April 1936

You wont be surprised to hear that I started the week here doing a little housepainting. I decided the dining room was really too shabby so I painted the walls a delicate pale green, & then the painted woodwork looked so dark I have begun to paint that too. Then Angelica and I decided that it would be fun to tackle the spare room. We have great plans for letting ourselves go in that, on the consideration that no visitor ever stays long enough to let it get on their nerves (or ought to do so) & we intend to introduce a fantastic note. But we havent started yet.

28 June 1936

There's been a good deal of rain here with very good results on the garden. At last I actually have a rose garden – enough roses to pick a bowl full & leave plenty on the trees. Walter works very hard & we just got him in time to save the garden this year even though he cant get it all in order – But we shall have plenty of flowers & a good many vegetables – & apples of course & I think plums. Next year I plan all sorts of things – more fruit trees & a hedge round the paddock which is now quite a respectable vegetable plot.

15 August 1936

Now for our news here – which is very tame & domestic & consists only of all the small Charleston happenings, about which you daydream – I know how one can do so – how heavenly all the smells & colours & clean easiness of life seem to me – as in fact they are. One result of the rain we have had is that when the sun does come out everything seems deliciously fresh. In fact it really has been finer this week & today has been quite hot. The garden is now a mass of flowers & as gay as possible with holly hocks & sweet peas & zinnias – tobacco & stocks smell strong in the evening. I often wander about in it at odd moments for the pleasure of the sights & smells.

EDWARD PLAYFAIR, *Memories of Charleston, from the Charleston Newsletter, no. 8, 1984*

Julian Bell was my great friend, and I used to spend week-ends with him at Charleston between 1927, when we got to know each other at Cambridge, and 1935, when he went to China. That is a long time ago, and my memories are precise rather than specific. They may owe their precision to all that I have read and seen since then, which tends to overlay direct memories . . .

Julian being Julian, my main memory is of incessant talk. On

38. Julian, Vanessa and Quentin Bell, Charleston, 1928

one occasion it went on till a winter dawn; why should one ever stop? Walks in moderation: Julian enjoyed them, but I was and am physically lazy. Meals I remember as always good, served by Grace, then unmarried and remarkably pretty. Vanessa was in charge, kind, reserved, beautiful and statuesque. She was then about fifty, but because she was my friend's mother and never tried to look younger than she was, I remember her as seeming older than that.

In spite of that winter night of talk, most of my memories are of hot weather and summer: is that not always so of places where one has been happy? The garden was a delight, and so were the Downs and even the shingly beach where we went to bathe *en bande* when a number of Julian's friends came to Charleston.

Clive and Duncan were benevolent presences; the young Angelica floated in and out: I have curiously few memories of Quentin at Charleston (many of him in Via Margutta in 1931) and I think he must have been elsewhere most of the time. But my most vivid and specific memories concentrate on the evenings, prolonged after the others had gone to bed into nights of talk, in the drawing room, with the death of Procris and that amiable dog on the wall, and Julian bouncing up and down and scuffing the cover of the sofa in growing excitement at his own multifarious thoughts and my modest objections.

I am not sure whether I ever stayed at Charleston in the years after Julian's departure and death; I think not, till my last visit there in 1941. I had just married, and the family were curious to meet my wife. We went down for a week-end: I enjoyed myself enormously, but she, who had never met any of them before, was rather frightened. Vanessa, Clive, Duncan and Quentin were there; Angelica (then living elsewhere, not far away, with Bunny) and Leonard came to Charleston to have a look; Lydia asked us over to Tilton so that my wife could meet Maynard. She found the conversation intimidating, except of course for Clive: he was always guaranteed to put anyone at ease.

The worst thing for her was something which I foresaw but failed to warn her about, though I should have, since she had never before had any contact with painters. As we went down I said to myself 'Is she paintable? I think so', but said nothing to her. At the first free moment, there she was on a dais, totally unprepared, being painted by Vanessa, Duncan and Quentin, fully believing in her innocence that they were looking at her as a person, and made duly shy by that belief. In fact, of course, at that time, she was only a model, something to paint, quite different from the girl at the dinner table in whom they took a very friendly interest. Duncan's portrait alone survived; he finished it and gave it to us as a wedding present. It remains on our wall as a delightful reminder of the Charleston painters.

ANGELICA GARNETT, *in her memoir Deceived with Kindness*

In September war was declared: we listened to Chamberlain on the radio in the garden at Charleston, which was glowing with the reds and oranges of the dying summer. The unreality of the occasion was in itself frightening . . .

VIRGINIA WOOLF, *in her Diary, 13 May 1940*

Duncan saw an air battle over Charleston – a silver pencil & a puff of smoke.

DAVID GARNETT, *in a letter to T. H. White, 11 November 1944*

Charleston . . . is a farmhouse on Lord Gage's estate with a walled garden, a pond in front of it & various additions in the form of studios, a pottery kiln etc at the back. Angelica was born in it & I lived in during the last 2 years of the last war. Its present inhabitants are Clive Bell, Vanessa Bell, Quentin Bell, Duncan Grant & at the moment Angelica, Amaryllis & myself. There is also Grace who with her husband & small son lives in what is called High Holborn which has a separate staircase leading out of the kitchen. The farm buildings & land are part of the farm nearest – Tilton – which is leased & run by Lord Keynes who is a very old friend of everyone here. He is the same as the Economic Consequences Keynes & is now in Washington with Lydia his wife. Life here follows a very ordered pattern. Clive shoots two days a week or more as a result of which we have lots of pheasants, partridges, hares & rabbits to eat & occasionally a snipe or duck. At other times, he sits in his own rooms & reads – at the moment G. Ferrero's History of Roman Empire in French. He goes off to see friends & gives lunch parties in London pretty often. Quentin who is about 34 is a painter & before the war a potter also. He has recently had his appendix out. He works half the day on the farm & paints in the afternoon. Angelica & he are painting a lovely young cock pheasant hung up against a looking glass. Their time limit is till Monday mid-day as we want to eat it on Monday evening. Quentin also reads a good deal: at the moment Ranke's history of Europe. Both Clive & Quentin are social & genial characters but in Clive's case it has become overlaid by a dogmatic

& rather noisy manner. No one sees anybody else in this house except at meals which last a long time. There is very decent draught beer & a tot of either rum or sherry or something in the evening – also a cigar provided by Clive . . .

Duncan is silent, & has a great many irons in the fire, – goes into Lewes to do lithographs – decorations for churches, conferences with Bishops about which we tease him. The only animals are a fine Tom Cat who lets Amaryllis pull his fur & tail, and a dog which doesn't belong here but to Lord Gage but which Clive always takes out shooting. He is an elderly Black Labrador . . .

However my description of Charleston has not begun. To begin with every room has been decorated & redecorated several times by Duncan & Vanessa during the last 28 years. The walls are covered with pictures varying from Cézannes & Matisses to almost anything or anybody. The seats of the chairs are in cross stitch & the curtains also made at home from their own designs. All this is now a half-seen background. Long rooted habits govern behaviour & thought as unconsciously & as rigidly as at the court of Louis XIV. There is therefore a sort of spiritual crystallisation which affects everyone – Duncan much the least. This can be at moments irritating, at other moments extraordinarily restful: – as restful as it would have been to live at Gryll Grange for example. Conversation at meals is more like Peacock than like any other writer.

JANIE BUSSY, *in a letter to Vanessa Bell, following her return to England from war-torn France*

It is wonderful to be in London again, but nevertheless how often do my thoughts hark back to Charleston. I don't know I should have faced life in general and London in particular without the peace and rest of Charleston first. No words can express my happiness at being with you all again so I just won't try to express it.

Visits to Charleston: Vanessa

Vanessa Bell was my grandmother. But I never called her Vanessa. I always called her Nessa. And although I always knew that Vanessa was her real name, I never heard anyone call her that within our family circle. She was rather proud that she was the first registered Vanessa. Her father, Sir Leslie Stephen, had been a great admirer of Jonathan Swift and had called her Vanessa after Esther Vanhomrigh (whom Swift had nick-named Vanessa), complementing the name of Vanessa's half-sister, Stella (the nick-name of Esther Vanhomrigh's rival). I remember that she told me, laughing, that some play, called *Clive and Vanessa*, which she said was of little merit, had once been staged in London. Duncan Grant, my grandfather, echoed her laughter and agreed that the play was atrocious.

When I knew her, Nessa was already an old woman. I can't remember not having known her. During the fifties, I frequently spent the school holidays at Charleston, often with my elder sister, Amaryllis. Those visits were a treat. For a child, it was an extraordinary treasure chest overflowing with familiar curiosities, beauty, ideas, people and jokes. It was a treasure chest that never emptied, however much it was rummaged about in. One of the greatest treats was that it never changed. It was always surprising, but it remained intrinsically the same.

Charleston had the most powerful identity of any place that I had known. It reeked of itself: of turpentine and toast, of apples, damp walls and garden flowers. The atmosphere was one of liberty and order, and of a strength which came from its being a house in which the inhabitants were happy. And they were happy, Nessa, Duncan and Clive, because they were working in conjunction with one another and harmoniously.

Charleston reeked of itself. It also reeked of Nessa's personality. For if Charleston had the most powerful identity of any place that I had ever known, Nessa had the strongest personality that I had ever encountered. I think that the essence of the house, this dichotomy between liberty and order, stemmed directly from her. Liberty and order were the roots of Nessa's character.

Nessa was an old woman, but even in her old age she was remarkably beautiful. Tall, thin, stooping with the elegance of a silver spoon, she had beautifully expressive eyes, the colour of the grey-blue beach pebbles which were scattered on the paths in the walled garden. Many of the clothes she wore, she made herself. The length of her skirts was long, the materials often from French or Italian markets, the colours dark and speckled with patterns like the aprons of Mediterranean peasant women. She was not a good dress-maker, but, in spite of her clothes being badly cut, she wore them with a grace which defied the cobbled stitches. Around her neck, she nearly always wore a pale scarf pinned with a brooch. There was one resembling a small snail made of lapis lazuli. Another was a cut garnet from which dangled three pink pendants. A third was green. It had been brought back from China and given to her by her eldest son, Julian. She wore several rings. One of these, too, was green, and also a present to her from Julian. He had picked that up in China, too.

Nessa was always the earliest down to breakfast. She did not eat much, for her habits were frugal. A slice of toast which she broke off slowly into little pieces, scraped thinly with butter and sprinkled with salt, and two cups of coffee. When Clive appeared, he would tap the barometer before sitting down opposite her at the painted, round table. Duncan was always the last down.

Breakfast over, Clive would disappear, either into his down-stairs book room which looked out through the magnolia leaves to the round pond, or up the green carpeted stairs to his book room* which over-looked the garden. We all thought Clive's quarters much more luxurious than anyone else's. They were.

When we stayed at Charleston, Amaryllis and I were always made to sit as models. We would follow Nessa and Duncan down the lengths of the passages to get to Duncan's studio. We were not altogether willing models and both of us charged our grandparents sixpence apiece for each hour that we endured. We were seldom painted in our ordinary clothes. In her bedroom, next to Duncan's studio, Nessa kept a huge painted cupboard which was filled with a fantastic assortment of coloured silks, discarded dresses and moth-eaten tapestries in which we were variously draped. I remember there was a vermilion velvet hat, like the head-dress of a Venetian doge, which was excruciatingly itchy for me to wear. Nessa usually sat down to paint. Her easel was infinitely more spindly, more rickety than Duncan's. She sat behind it, mixing the colours on her palette, glancing first at us and then at the portrait, gently stabbing the canvas, so that, posing somewhat uneasily and swathed in remnants on the model's throne, one could see the back of her canvas quiver from the impressions she made on it. The glances she sent across the room were extraordinarily intimate and reassuring: an observant nod, an amused smile, in order to encourage us to keep still.

Like all children, we loved to hear about the past. And while Nessa and Duncan painted us, they would tell us stories about their youth: about the Olden Days. Nessa once told me that the first thing she could remember was seeing a mouse running across her cradle where she had been brought up in Hyde Park Gate. She told us of sailing wooden toy boats in the Round Pond in Kensington Gardens; of the terrible difficulties she had in lacing

---

* the downstairs book room is now known as Clive Bell's study, that upstairs as the library.

up the buttons on the black boots she had to wear and how she hated them. She spoke of the family holidays by the Cornish seaside. She said that on several occasions she had seen Queen Victoria being driven in a carriage drawn by cream-coloured ponies. She made me laugh at her anecdotes about Aunt Annie (Thackeray's daughter), entrancing me with handed down tales of the goings-on at Little Holland House. She spoke of the beauty of her half-sister, Stella; of the stillness of her mother, Julia; of the love she had had for her brother Thoby; of her half-brother George, who was so greedy that he ate plum cake spread with butter and with jam. And to us, these dead relations were like characters from an unwritten serial story; half-mythical creatures made alive by the intimate details which Nessa imparted to them.

As well as conversation, there was music. Beethoven, Mozart, Debussy were favourites. These we listened to on the Third Programme on the wireless. But never God. Amaryllis and I delighted in trying to torment her by switching on the Home Service to tune into *The Daily Service*. But Nessa was adamant. She refused the intrusion of hymns and sermons into the studio and switched off God with authority.

Sometimes, we were permitted to read while we sat, so long as we held our positions after turning the pages. Often, Amaryllis would read aloud. She read aloud very well, which was a gift she shared with Nessa. She read *The Mill on the Floss*, *The Torrents of Spring*, *My Grandmothers and I*. But mainly, she read aloud from the works of Miss Charlotte M. Yonge, a nineteenth-century romantic novelist, whose works are concerned chiefly with re-ligion, love and death. Nessa and her sister, Virginia, had been brought up on them. Amaryllis and I inherited their addiction for the writings of Miss Yonge and we enjoyed them for very much the same reasons. We adored the death scenes. We relished them. They made us cry and they made us laugh. And Nessa laughed too. She had a strangely mellow cackle; the amused hoot of a tawny owl.

Like all models, Amaryllis and I insisted on rests as our rights. During the rests, we would curl up on the studio floor in front of the painted tiles by the pither stove. There, we would extract the pins and needles from our aching limbs and listen to *Mrs Dale's Diary*. Grace Higgens, the much-loved cook, brought our elevenses into the studio on a tray. Our elevenses consisted of milk in ochre-coloured mugs, which were decorated with white lilies by Duncan, and digestive biscuits. The goings-on of the Dales intrigued us all almost as much as the death scenes in the novels of Charlotte Yonge, although for rather different reasons. After the fifteen-minute episode had ended to the twinkling tones of its signature tune, all four of us would speculate and elaborate wildly upon the curious lives of Mrs Maggs, Mrs Dale and her scandalous sister, Sally, dwelling, as they did, in Virginia Water.

Nessa was an economical woman. But one never felt stinted at Charleston. The food was good, entirely owing to Grace Higgens, who was an excellent cook. The wine was good, too, owing to Clive and to Duncan, who enjoyed baiting each other with a teasing rivalry over the contents of the cellar. But Nessa held the household accounts on a short rein. She had been brought up to it, and it was a habit which never left her.

Luncheon consisted almost invariably of cold ham which Nessa would carve up into translucent pink slithers, baked potatoes and pickled walnuts. Duncan, having shambled out into the garden for herbs, would dress the salad. The grown-ups drank a bottle of dark stout each at lunch. The wine, they drank at dinner. We had pudding once a day, at lunch but never at dinner. I think that was really one of Nessa's ways of teasing Duncan. She did not have a sweet tooth and Duncan had a passion for puddings. He was never allowed to forget that once, as a child in India, he had stolen down during the night and had been discovered devouring an entire batch of lemon curd tarts. Junket and Queen of Puddings were our favourites. While Nessa and Duncan and Clive sipped their black coffee, Nessa gave us *canards*. The duck, a lump of white sugar, would be sent for a sail in a silver teaspoon boat across the dark waters of the black coffee in her painted blue cup. Very gently, the silver boat capsized. The snow-white duck became stained with the brown liquid. Nessa would lift the spoon to our gaping mouths, and then we gobbled up our ducks.

The afternoons at Charleston were more relaxed from a working point of view than the mornings. If it was fine weather, Clive would take Amaryllis and me out for a walk with his dogs. Sometimes, we went with Duncan or with my Uncle Quentin, if he was there. Nessa scarcely ever went out for walks.

If it rained during the afternoon, Amaryllis and I would often spend the time between lunch and tea with Nessa in her studio. For although Nessa and Duncan very often painted the same subjects and shared their studios, they both had separate ones, and referred to them as such. Duncan's studio was downstairs. Nessa's studio was at the very top of the house. When Amaryllis and I were very young, we passed the time there making dolls' clothes from scraps out of Nessa's sewing rag-bag. She was a great hoarder, a magpie, and so there was a plethora of odds and ends for us to turn into ball-gowns for our dolls. Nessa entered into our childhood world of fantasy with relish, and she had a delightful and comic sense of invention. One of our greatest pleasures, after the dolls had been clothed in their furbelows, was to pretend that they were languishing for love of the teddy bear, to make them pine away and give them the typhoid, the malaria, and the fatal, fatal fever. When they had the fever, Nessa would inoculate them by jabbing them in the arm with a long darning needle. Occasionally, we were allowed to read *The Hyde Park Gate News*, a family news-paper written by the Stephen children, which was kept on the floor underneath a shelf in her studio.

It was a small room, an attic, with a beautiful view extending beyond the walled garden to fields and, to the left, a glimpse of Compton Wood. I think that it is indicative of her character that, while she slept downstairs in a room opening through French windows onto the walled garden, she worked at the top of the house. I believe that the view was essential to her. She needed light. She needed distant horizons. She was a woman with very clear views of her own. For Nessa could shock, astonish, leave one giddy with her point of view. She was the first person to show me that grown-ups were not necessarily pillars of wisdom; that they were as vulnerable and as questionable as I was myself. She taught me that human beings, whatever their age or authority, should be treated as equals. She was the first true revolutionary whom I ever had the luck to know. Being with her, alone in the upper studio, was sometimes like looking at life from the height of a Campanile tower.

I remember, once, when she was painting me in the upper studio, I was being more than usually restless. We were by ourselves. She asked me what the matter was. I told her the truth. My trouble was my hair. My father's sense of aesthetics still retained more than a vestige of the neo-pagan attitudes which he had held during the early years of the century. All four of his daughters had long, wild and tangled locks. I don't think that my sisters were bothered by this. But my bedraggled appearance made me miserable. I longed for a conventional fifties' bob. Nessa probably agreed with my father that long hair was more becoming than a bob. But that was not the point. The point was that one had the right to express oneself freely. And that, she understood. She was delighted by my rebellious feelings. She made an appointment for me at the barber's shop in Lewes, and the next afternoon she sat and watched while I had all my hair snipped up to my ears in the company of red-cheeked farmers having a short back and sides and a shave. I have never understood why we went to the barber's shop instead of a ladies' hairdresser. The choice was typically curious of her.

Tea was at five o'clock and, at about half past four, Nessa would go downstairs into the kitchen and put on the kettle. The kitchen was large, ill lit and rather gloomy. It had a concrete floor. Sometimes Nessa would make scones. She would stand at the kitchen table, remove her rings and hoik them up onto a nail above the sink, sift flour through her long fingers and let it drift into the pudding basin. She never spilled the ingredients; never made a mess. The recipe she used was not extravagant. It required a minimum of butter and lacked varnish of egg-yolk. They were plain scones and they were very good.

As we grew older, Amaryllis and I were allowed to stay up for dinner instead of being given an early supper. On these occasions, we both paraded in fantastic evening dress concocted from curtains, lengths of Omega cloth, Nessa's night-gowns, feathers, flowers and finery borrowed from her jewel boxes. Then we pretended that we were grand ladies, duchesses, courtesans and curates' daughters. We flirted outrageously with Duncan and Clive. On one occasion, we went so far as to have a double wedding. Amaryllis married Clive. I married Duncan. This curious wedding party took place one sunny afternoon and it was held in the piazza by the pond beneath the large apple tree. Nessa officiated as high priestess. Then we all went back into the dining room and ate up one of Grace's seed cakes for tea.

They were delightful evenings. Our childish follies were entered into, enlivened and bettered by the company which we kept. For Clive was a witty and erudite conversationalist of great charm and intelligence. Duncan was an enchanting individual. Nessa loved them both. She gazed from one to another with her beautiful blue-grey eyes and let the smoke drift slowly from the Gauloise which she smoked with her after-dinner coffee. At intervals, she would murmur, 'How absurd.'

If Nessa reminds me of any woman out of literature, it is of Diotima of Mantinea. She was a woman of principle. She also possessed an extraordinary sense of humour, a capacity to mock and a rare gift for intimacy.

Visits to Charleston were a treat. It is still a treat for me to remember my grandmother.

Biographical Notes

HELEN ANREP (1885–1965), *née* Maitland, studied music in Europe and associated with the circle of Augustus John and Henry Lamb. In 1917, she married the Russian mosaicist Boris von Anrep (responsible for the pavements in the entrance hall of the National Gallery, London, where many of the gods and goddesses are portraits of the Bloomsbury circle) and with him had two children, Anastasia and Igor. From 1926 until his death, she lived with Roger Fry. A frequent visitor to Charleston, she was often painted by Vanessa Bell and Duncan Grant.

FREDERICK ASHTON (b. 1904), choreographer and dancer. Born in Ecuador, he was to become founder-choreographer to the Royal Ballet and visited Charleston through his friendship with Lydia Keynes.

BARBARA BAGENAL (1891–1984), *née* Hiles, painter, gardener and botanist, studied at the Slade School, 1913–14, where she made friends with Dora Carrington, and married Nicholas Bagenal in 1918. A frequent visitor to Charleston for over half a century, she was devoted to Vanessa Bell and, particularly, to Clive Bell, and made several bequests to the Charleston Trust.

GEORGE BARNE (1882–19?), painter, elected to London Group in 1922 and a member of the London Artists' Association. Lived mainly in Paris; published *The Three Orders of Perspective* (1928).

KEITH BAYNES (1887–1972), painter, studied in France and England. Frequently exhibited alongside his friends Vanessa Bell and Duncan Grant in the London Artists' Association and the London Group.

CLIVE BELL (1881–1964), art and literary critic, author of *Civilization* (1928) and *Old Friends* (1956); coined the term 'significant form' in his book *Art* (1914) and supported many of Roger Fry's ideas on aesthetics. Married

Vanessa Stephen in 1907 and, although he maintained a separate establishment at 50 Gordon Square, London, during the inter-war years, shared Charleston with Duncan Grant and Vanessa Bell until his death.

JULIAN BELL (1908–37), elder son of Vanessa and Clive Bell, poet. Appointed Professor of English at the University of Wuhan, near Hankow, China in 1935; killed two years later while serving as an ambulance driver during the Spanish Civil War. His *Essays, Poems and Letters* were published posthumously in 1938.

(ANNE) OLIVIER BELL (b. 1916), *née* Popham, married Quentin Bell in 1952; they have a son, Julian, and two daughters, Virginia and Cressida. Editor of *The Diary of Virginia Woolf, 1915–41*, and serves on the Charleston Trust. Frequently painted by Vanessa Bell and Duncan Grant as well as by artists of the Euston Road School.

QUENTIN BELL (b. 1910), younger son of Vanessa and Clive Bell, painter, potter, sculptor, biographer of Virginia Woolf, art historian, Emeritus Professor of the History and Theory of Art, Sussex University, and first chairman of the Charleston Trust. In 1952, he married Anne Olivier Popham.

VANESSA ('NESSA') BELL (1879–1961), *née* Stephen, painter, designer of fabrics (for Allan Walton), carpets, embroidery and ceramics (for Wedgwood and others), and painter of pottery, decorative tiles and furniture. She did woodcuts, some of which illustrate her sister Virginia Woolf's books, and designed jackets for The Hogarth Press. She also designed for the ballet. A co-director of the Omega Workshops, 1913–19, with Roger Fry and Duncan Grant, she was between the wars involved in the London Artists' Association and the London Group. From 1949–59 she sat on the committee of the Abbey Trust Fund for mural painting. The elder daughter of Julia Jackson and Leslie Stephen, she married Clive Bell in 1907 and had two sons, Julian and Quentin. After a love affair with Roger Fry, she lived with Duncan Grant, with whom she moved to Charleston in 1916, and had a daughter, Angelica, by him two years later. She lived and worked with Grant there and in London until her death.

GEORGE BERGEN (1903–84), painter of Russian and Dutch origins who spent much of his life in the United States of America. Met Duncan Grant in 1930 and held his first one-artist exhibition in London at the Lefevre Gallery (catalogue preface by David Garnett) in 1932.

FRANCIS ('FRANKIE') BIRRELL (1889–1935), son of Augustine Birrell, literary critic and biographer, frequent visitor to Charleston. With David

Garnett, he worked with a Quaker relief unit in France during World War I, rebuilding houses in the Marne; they later started a bookshop together near Gordon Square frequented by the Bloomsbury circle.

ANTHONY BLUNT (1907–80), art historian; a Cambridge contemporary of Julian Bell, with whom he first visited Charleston; later Professor of Art History at University of London, Director of the Courtauld Institute, London, Surveyor of, then adviser for the Queen's Pictures, and known as 'the fourth man' in the Philby–Burgess–Maclean spy case.

DOROTHY BUSSY (1866–1960), *née* Strachey, writer and translator (particularly of Gide) and author of *Olivia* (1949). Elder sister of Lytton Strachey, in 1903 she married Simon Bussy and had a daughter, Janie. Lived principally at La Souco, Roquebrune, Alpes Maritimes.

JANE SIMONE ('JANIE') BUSSY (1906–60), painter, translator and intellectual. Active in the French Resistance during World War II, which she spent with her parents, Dorothy and Simon, in France. Exhibited work at the Leicester Galleries.

SIMON BUSSY (1870–1954), French painter, fellow student and friend of Henri Matisse and sometime teacher of Duncan Grant, cousin of his wife, Dorothy. Spent most of his time in France, but also worked in England and Scotland.

DORA CARRINGTON (1892–1932), painter; known usually only by her surname. She lived with Lytton Strachey from 1917, the year of her only recorded visit to Charleston. Her post-war marriage to Ralph Partridge expanded the ménage, but she remained devoted to Strachey and stayed with him until his death in 1932. She committed suicide seven weeks later.

PIERRE-EUGÈNE CLAIRIN (1897–1980), French painter and lithographer; studied under Serusier; professor of lithography at the Ecole des Beaux-Arts, Paris, 1957–67; old friend of the Bells and Duncan Grant.

ANGUS DAVIDSON (1898–1980), writer and translator; worked at The Hogarth Press and as secretary to the London Artists' Association, of which his brother Douglas, painter and designer, was a member; published *Edward Lear* (1938); close friend of Duncan Grant and Vanessa Bell, and frequent visitor to Charleston.

ANDRÉ DERAIN (1880–1954), French painter and designer and leading Fauvist. Derain's work became known in England through the advocacy of Roger Fry and especially Clive Bell, who was a friend of the artist from 1918 onwards.

HENRI DOUCET (1883–1915), French painter who paid several visits to England between 1912 and 1914; was painted by Duncan Grant and Vanessa Bell and worked for Roger Fry at the Omega Workshops. Killed while fighting in World War I.

THOMAS STEARNS ELIOT (1888–1965), American-born poet, critic and dramatist, winner of the 1948 Nobel Prize for Literature. Settled in England, he was employed by Lloyds Bank from 1917 until he joined the publishers Faber and Faber in 1925, and thereafter devoted himself to writing and editing. Friend of Leonard and Virginia Woolf, who published *The Waste Land* in 1923.

FREDERICK ETCHELLS (1886–1973), painter; from 1911 closely associated with Roger Fry and Duncan Grant and later with the Omega Workshops and the Rebel Art Centre. After World War I, concentrated almost entirely on architecture and was architectural adviser for the Berwick Church murals in Sussex, created by Vanessa Bell, Duncan Grant and others.

JESSICA ('JESSIE') ETCHELLS (1893–1933), painter, sister of Frederick Etchells; exhibited at Second Post-Impressionist Exhibition, 1912, and worked briefly the following year at the Omega Workshops, but gave up painting on her marriage to David Leacock in 1915.

(EDWARD) MORGAN FORSTER (1879–1970), novelist and critic. His last novel, *A Passage to India*, was published in 1924, but he continued to write fiction, biography and criticism, and was an active figure in support of liberal causes, the first president of the National Council for Civil Liberties. Made his home at King's College, Cambridge, where he had become an honorary fellow in 1946; awarded the Order of Merit in 1969. First visited Charleston in 1919 and occasionally thereafter; painted there by Vanessa Bell and Duncan Grant, 1940.

OTHON FRIESZ (1879–1949), French painter briefly associated with Fauvism; friend of Roger Fry and Clive Bell.

ROGER FRY (1866–1934), art critic and painter; studied in London and at the Académie Julian in Paris; organised the First and Second Post-Impressionist exhibitions in London in 1910 and 1912 and the next year founded the Omega Workshops; publications include *Vision and Design* (1920) and *Cézanne* (1927); Slade Professor of Fine Art at Cambridge, 1933–34. His marriage in 1896 to the painter Helen Coombe ended tragically when she became incurably insane and was institutionalised; in 1911 he fell in love with Vanessa Bell, and never wholly out of it; from 1926 until his death he lived with Helen Anrep and was a frequent and much loved visitor to Charleston.

NICOLAS GALANIS (1882–1966), painter and printmaker born in Greece; French citizen, 1914; made illustrations to Rolland, Gide, Valéry and others.

ANGELICA GARNETT (b. 1918), *née* Bell, only child of Vanessa Bell and Duncan Grant, painter and writer, author of *Mosaics* (1967). A member of the Charleston Trust, she was born in the house on Christmas Day. Married David Garnett in 1942 and had four daughters, Amaryllis, Henrietta, Nerissa and Frances. Her youth at Charleston is recounted in *Deceived with Kindness* (1984).

DAVID ('BUNNY') GARNETT (1892–1981), author, publisher and some-time literary editor of the *New Statesman*; his best-known novel is *Lady into Fox* (1921). The son of Edward and Constance Garnett (the translator of nineteenth-century Russian novelists), he moved as a conscientious objector during World War I to Charleston with Vanessa Bell and Duncan Grant, with whom he worked as a farm labourer – experiences described in his *Flowers of the Forest* (1955). Married Ray Marshall (Frances Partridge's sister) in 1921 and, two years after her death in 1940, Angelica Bell.

HENRIETTA GARNETT (b. 1945), author, second daughter of David and Angelica Garnett. Frequent visitor to Charleston in the 1950s, where she was painted by Vanessa Bell and Duncan Grant. Her novel *Family Skeletons* was published in 1986.

ABEL GERBAUD (1888–1954), French painter of landscapes and seascapes.

MARCEL GIMOND (1891–1961), French sculptor and draughtsman; briefly studio assistant to Renoir; follower of Maillol. Through friendship with Roger Fry made busts of Fry, his daughter Pamela, and Vanessa Bell.

SYLVIA GOSSE (1881–1968), painter and etcher, daughter of Sir Edmund Gosse; closely associated with Sickert and his circle.

DUNCAN GRANT (1885–1978), painter and designer, cousin of Lytton Strachey and his numerous siblings, with whom he spent much of his youth. Studied with Jacques-Emile Blanche in Paris before returning to London, where he was a co-director of the Omega Workshops and a member of the London Artists' Association and the London Group. Persuaded Maynard Keynes to ask the government for money to buy pictures at the Degas sale in Paris, 1918, many of which are in the National Gallery, London. Duncan Grant himself was given two exhibitions at the Tate Gallery during his lifetime. Designed textiles, rugs and embroidery, painted ceramics and furniture, also murals and interior decoration. Did woodcuts and illustrations as well as several theatre designs. From 1914 he lived and worked with Vanessa Bell, moving with her in 1916 to Charleston, where in 1918 she gave birth to his daughter, Angelica. Although he maintained a London studio, the farmhouse remained his home and principal studio until his death over sixty years later.

ETHEL GRANT (1863–1947), *née* McNeil, wife of Major Bartle Grant 1860–1924) and mother of Duncan Grant. A gifted needlewoman, she carried out designs by Duncan Grant and Vanessa Bell in *gros point*, several examples of which are to be seen at Charleston.

ROGER DE GREY (b. 1918), painter, President of the Royal Academy of Arts from 1985; visitor to Charleston in the 1950s.

ALICE HALICKA (1894–1975), Polish painter of the Ecole de Paris; married to Louis Marcoussis; author of *Hier (Souvenirs)* (1946).

NINA HAMNETT (1890–1956), painter, writer and bohemian; employed by Roger Fry at the Omega Workshops.

HENRI HAYDEN (1883–1970), French painter of Polish origin briefly associated with Cubism; later work includes still life and landscape.

(JOHN) NICHOLAS HENDERSON (b. 1919), diplomat, lastly as British Ambassador to Washington. Stayed at Charleston as one of Marjorie Strachey's summer-school pupils.

GRACE HIGGENS (1904–83), *née* Germany, born in Norfolk, she joined Vanessa Bell's household when she was sixteen, finally becoming cook-housekeeper at Charleston, where she lived with her husband, Walter, and son, Peter John, until her retirement in 1970.

MARY HUTCHINSON (1889–1977), *née* Barnes, a cousin of the Stracheys. Married the barrister St John Hutchinson in 1910 and later had a long love affair with Clive Bell. Early visitor to Charleston and patron of Duncan Grant and Vanessa Bell; author of *Fugitive Pieces* (1927).

AUGUSTUS JOHN (1878–1961), celebrated English portrait painter and brother of Gwen John; met Duncan Grant in Paris in 1907 and Clive and Vanessa Bell shortly afterwards in London; maintained cordial professional relations with Vanessa Bell and Duncan Grant for many years.

LYDIA KEYNES (1892–1981), *née* Lopokova, Russian ballerina. After training at the Imperial School of Ballet in St Petersburg, she travelled to London in 1918 with Diaghilev's *Ballets Russes* and, from 1921, remained at Maynard Keynes's persuasion; she married him four years later, continuing her career on the London stage both as dancer and actress. After Keynes's death she stayed on at their home, Tilton, near Charleston.

(JOHN) MAYNARD KEYNES (1882–1946), economist, writer, Fellow and Bursar of King's College, Cambridge. The British Treasury's chief representative during the Paris Peace Conference after World War I, he resigned over the settlement being imposed on Germany and wrote *The Economic Consequences of the Peace* (1919) at Charleston (where he was living as an intimate friend of Duncan Grant and Vanessa Bell); this was followed by several seminal works on economics. After his marriage in 1925 to Lydia Lopokova, settled at Tilton, the property neighbouring Charleston; he was created Baron Keynes of Tilton in 1942.

HENRY LAMB (1883–1960), painter; close early friend of Lytton Strachey and Lady Ottoline Morrell and a member of Vanessa Bell's exhibiting society, The Friday Club, from 1905–8; made pencil drawings of Clive Bell and Duncan Grant and portraits of Strachey and Leonard Woolf.

MICHEL LARIONOV (1881–1964), Russian painter and theatre designer who, with his wife, the painter Nathalie Goncharova, settled in Paris in 1914; both closely associated with Diaghilev's *Ballets Russes*; exhibited theatre designs at the Omega Workshops, 1919.

EDWARD LE BAS (1904–66), painter and collector; close friend of Duncan Grant and Vanessa Bell with whom he painted in Europe in 1946 (Dieppe) and in 1955 (Asolo). Owned many works by the two artists and posed for the figure of Christ crucified in Grant's panel in Berwick Church, Sussex.

JOHN LEHMANN (1907-87), poet, critic, editor and publisher; worked at The Hogarth Press. Brother of the writer Rosamond Lehmann and the actress Beatrix, he became at Cambridge a close friend of Julian Bell, whom he visited at Charleston.

CONSTANCE LLOYD, English painter who spent most of her life in Paris; studied in London under Simon Bussy; became a friend of Gwen John in Paris and introduced Duncan Grant to her in 1907; exhibited paintings and book illustrations at the Salon d'Automne; remained on friendly terms with Grant for many years.

DESMOND MACCARTHY (1877–1952), author and critic and literary editor of *New Statesman*, 1920–27, and subsequently senior literary critic on *The*

Sunday Times; president of the English P.E.N. club; knighted 1951. With his wife, Molly – they were married in 1906 – a frequent visitor to Charleston, where he was painted by Vanessa Bell and Duncan Grant and sculpted by Quentin Bell.

MARY ('MOLLY') MACCARTHY (1882–1953), *née* Warre-Cornish, writer and wife of Desmond MacCarthy, with whom she had three children, Michael, Rachel and Dermod.

MEMOIR CLUB. Met for the first time on 4 March 1920 and continued to the early 1960s; initially composed of members of Old Bloomsbury, who would dine together and hear autobiographical papers read by two or sometimes three members. Meetings usually took place in London with dinner in a restaurant; there were occasional meetings at Charleston and Tilton. For over twenty-five years, from its inception, the Club's secretary was Molly MacCarthy; its last secretary was Frances Partridge. Many papers such as those read by Leonard Woolf, David Garnett and Clive Bell later formed part of their published memoirs.

RAYMOND MORTIMER (1895–1980), man of letters; literary editor of *New Statesman and Nation*, 1935–47; critic for *The Times Literary Supplement* and *The Sunday Times*; author of *Duncan Grant* (1944). Close friend of Clive Bell and frequent visitor to Charleston; his London flat was decorated by Duncan Grant and Vanessa Bell in 1925.

JOHN NASH (1893–1977), painter and illustrator, brother of Paul Nash; took to painting after World War I and exhibited with the London Group.

JEAN OBERLÉ (1900–61), French illustrator and painter; author of *La Vie d'Artiste* (1956).

RODERIC O'CONOR (1860–1940), Irish painter who spent most of his life in France; influenced by Gauguin and the Pont-Aven group from 1892; close friend of Clive Bell from 1904 and through him met Roger Fry, Duncan Grant, Derain and others.

OMEGA WORKSHOPS. A co-operative workshop-cum-showroom at 33 Fitzroy Square, London, founded by Roger Fry and run by him from 1913 to 1919 for the production of painted furniture, textiles, ceramics, artefacts and mural decoration. Vanessa Bell and Duncan Grant were co-directors. Most of the leading avant-garde painters of the period were employed there at one time or another. Notable Omega products at Charleston include the dining-room chairs, the lily-pond table in Keynes's bedroom and the folding screen in Vanessa Bell's bedroom and some ceramics.

FRANCES PARTRIDGE (b. 1900), *née* Marshall, author of *A Pacifist's War* (1978) and other memoirs. After leaving Newnham College, Cambridge, worked at Birrell and Garnett's bookshop in Bloomsbury; later worked on the Greville Memoirs with Lytton Strachey and Ralph Partridge, whom she married after the death of his first wife, Carrington. A particular friend of Clive Bell, she often visited Charleston.

ROLAND PENROSE (1900–1984), artist and arts administrator, organiser of International Surrealist Exhibition, 1936, founder and head for many years of Institute of Contemporary Arts, London. Lived at Chiddingly, not far from Charleston.

EDWARD PLAYFAIR (b. 1909), civil servant, and one time chairman of the Trustees of the National Gallery, London. A Cambridge contemporary of Julian Bell, with whom his first visits to Charleston were made, he married Dr Mary Rae in 1941.

WILLIAM PLOMER (1903–73), poet and novelist. After living in South Africa and Japan, he settled, in 1929, in London, where his books – including his most famous, *Turbott Wolfe* (1926) – were published by Leonard and Virginia Woolf, of whom he became a friend.

FREDERICK J. PORTER (1883–1944), painter, born in New Zealand but lived and worked in England; fellow exhibitor with Vanessa Bell and Duncan Grant in the London Group and the London Artists' Association.

MARY POTTER (1900–83), painter; elected to the London Group, 1938; lived in Aldeburgh, Suffolk.

HERBERT READ (1893–1968), art historian, critic and poet. Stayed at Charleston in 1935 with his first wife, Evelyn Roff, and their family when the Bell ménage was absent.

PIERRE ROY (1880–1949), French surrealist painter whose work was probably introduced to Clive Bell by Boris Anrep, Roy's closest friend.

ELLIOTT SEABROOKE (1886–1950), painter; exhibitor with Vanessa Bell's Friday Club and with the London Group, of which he was president, 1943–48.

RICHARD SHONE (b. 1949), writer on art and Associate Editor of the *Burlington Magazine*; author of *Bloomsbury Portraits* (1976). As a friend of Duncan Grant, he first visited Charleston in 1965 and was a frequent visitor thereafter.

WALTER RICHARD SICKERT (1860–1942), English painter and critic; subject of Virginia Woolf's *Walter Sickert: A Conversation* (1934), he had a studio at 8 Fitzroy Street (subsequently Duncan Grant's). Founded the Fitzroy Group (1907) and the Camden Town Group (1911), which later formed a prominent part of the London Group. One of the most influential figures in modern British art, he painted Lydia Lopokova and, in 1930, drew Quentin Bell. His work was owned by many of the Bloomsbury circle of friends.

MATTHEW SMITH (1879–1959), painter, studied in England and in Paris; elected to the London Group, 1916; a friend of Duncan Grant and Vanessa Bell from the early 1920s, he painted a portrait of Angelica Bell in 1957–8.

ETHEL SMYTH (1858–1944), composer (she studied in the circle of Brahms in Leipzig), author, suffragist and feminist – an intimate friend of Virginia Woolf.

ADRIAN STEPHEN (1883–1948), younger brother of Vanessa Bell and Virginia Woolf, doctor, psychoanalyst and a perpetrator of *The Dreadnought Hoax* (1936). In 1914 married Karin Costelloe, sister of Oliver Strachey's wife Ray, and had two daughters, Ann and Judith, who were often at Charleston.

LYTTON STRACHEY (1880–1932), critic and biographer, author of *Eminent Victorians* (1918) and *Queen Victoria* (1921). A cousin of Duncan Grant and a contemporary of Clive Bell at Cambridge, he was among Charleston's favourite visitors, making more or less annual trips there from 1917 onwards.

MARJORIE STRACHEY (1882–1964), author and teacher, notably of her summer school at Charleston. One of Lytton Strachey's many siblings, she wrote several books, among them *Mazzini, Garibaldi and Cavour*, which The Hogarth Press published in 1937.

OLIVER STRACHEY (1874–1960), an elder brother of Lytton Strachey. After studying music with Lechetitsky in Vienna and working in India, was employed as a codebreaker for the Foreign Office. Had a daughter, Julia, by his first wife, Ruby Mayer, and in 1911 married Ray Costelloe (sister of Karin, Adrian Stephen's wife), with whom he had two children: Christopher, who went to Marjorie Strachey's summer school at Charleston, and Barbara, author of *Remarkable Relations* (1980).

SAXON SYDNEY-TURNER (1880–1962), erudite, musical and taciturn contemporary of Clive Bell, Lytton Strachey and Leonard Woolf at Cambridge and closely associated with early Bloomsbury. A civil servant all his working life, he first visited Charleston in 1917.

STEPHEN TOMLIN (1901–37), sculptor; abandoned law studies at Oxford to work with Frank Dobson. In 1927 married Julia Strachey, writer and niece of Lytton Strachey. Made portrait busts of, among others, Duncan Grant, Lytton Strachey and Virginia Woolf; the last, modelled in 1931, is now at Charleston, where he was a frequent visitor.

CHARLES VILDRAC (1882–1964), poet, dramatist and manager of the Galerie Vildrac in Paris, which showed work by Fry, Grant and Bell alongside their French contemporaries; friendship with Fry and the Charleston artists dated from 1911.

ALLAN WALTON (1891–1948), painter, decorator, textile designer and manufacturer; his textile company produced many designs during the 1930s by Vanessa Bell and Duncan Grant – examples of these can still be seen at Charleston, and some have been reproduced by Laura Ashley for sale in their shops – as well as by Frank Dobson, Cedric Morris, Keith Baynes and other artists.

ELIZABETH WATSON, painter, secretary of the Artists' International Association in the late 1930s; friend of Quentin Bell. At her 1940 Calmann Gallery exhibition in London, she showed several works depicting Cassis and its surroundings painted at La Bergère, the French farmhouse where Vanessa Bell and her family spent part of the summer.

EDWARD WOLFE (1897–1982), painter; born in Johannesburg, he studied at the Slade School and worked with Roger Fry at the Omega Workshops. Frequently exhibited alongside Vanessa Bell and Duncan Grant in the London Artists' Association and the London Group. He first visited Charleston in 1918 and painted there in 1919.

LEONARD WOOLF (1880–1969), author, editor and publisher. Worked in the Ceylon Civil Service, 1904–11, and, the year after his return, married Virginia Stephen; with her, founded The Hogarth Press, publishing, among many others, Sigmund Freud, T. S. Eliot, E. M. Forster, Vita Sackville-West and Laurens van der Post. Literary editor of the *Nation & Athenaeum*, 1923–29, and on the board of the *New Statesman*, he also wrote two novels and a political work, *After the Deluge* (2 vols., 1931, 1939) – he was, in addition, involved in the League of Nations and various parliamentary committees – and five volumes of autobiography. 'Discovered' Charleston in 1916 while living at Asham nearby.

VIRGINIA WOOLF (1882–1941), *née* Stephen, novelist and critic. Sister of Vanessa Bell, she married Leonard Woolf in 1912 and together they founded The Hogarth Press at Richmond, Surrey, before moving to London. She divided her time between there and Sussex, where she lived first at Asham, then at Monks House, Rodmell, both a few miles from Charleston, which she visited constantly with Leonard Woolf, sometimes bringing her own house-guests. She suffered periodic nervous breakdowns, and drowned herself in 1941, not long after finishing the last of her nine novels, *Between the Acts*.

EVE NELSON YOUNGER, descendant of Nelson and daughter of a doctor. Fellow pupil of Angelica Bell's at Rose Paul's dame school (or class of three) in Mecklenburgh Square, London. She took part in the original production of *Freshwater*, Virginia Woolf's comedy based on Julia Margaret Cameron, the photographer and her great-aunt, and full of family jokes, which was rehearsed at Charleston and first performed in 1935 in Vanessa Bell's studio in Fitzroy Street, London.

Further Reading

DECORATIVE ARTS AND THEORY

Anscombe, Isabelle, *Omega and After: Bloomsbury and the Decorative Arts* (London, 1981)

Bell, Clive, *Art* (London, 1914)

Bell, Quentin, *Bloomsbury* (new ed., London, 1986)

— *Techniques of Terracotta* (London, 1983)

Collins, Judith, *The Omega Workshops* (London, 1983)

Fry, Roger, *Vision and Design* (London, 1920)

The Omega Workshops, 1913–19: Decorative Arts of Bloomsbury (catalogue of an exhibition at the Crafts Council Gallery, 1984), (London, 1983)

Shone, Richard, *Bloomsbury Portraits: Vanessa Bell, Duncan Grant and their Circle* (Oxford, 1976)

— and Collins, Judith, *Duncan Grant: Designer* (exhibition catalogue; Liverpool, 1980)

Watney, Simon, *English Post-Impressionism* (London, 1980)

PRINCIPAL BIOGRAPHIES, JOURNALS AND LETTERS OF THOSE MOST INTIMATELY CONNECTED WITH CHARLESTON

Bell, Clive, *Old Friends* (London, 1956)

Bell, Julian, *Essays, Poems & Letters*, ed. Quentin Bell (London, 1938)

Bell, Quentin, *Roger Fry* (Leeds, 1965)

— *Virginia Woolf: A Biography* (new ed., London, 1982)

Fry, Roger, *Duncan Grant* (London, 1924)

— *Letters*, ed. Denys Sutton (2 vols, London, 1972)

Garnett, Angelica, *Deceived with Kindness* (London, 1984)

Garnett, David, *The Familiar Faces* (London, 1962)

— *Flowers of the Forest* (London, 1955)

— *The Golden Echo* (London, 1953)

— *Great Friends* (London, 1979)

Holroyd, Michael, *Lytton Strachey* (London, 1971)

Skidelsky, Robert, *John Maynard Keynes, Vol. 1: Hopes Betrayed, 1883–1920*, (London, 1983)

Spalding, Frances, *Vanessa Bell* (London, 1983)

— *Roger Fry* (London, 1980)

Spater, George & Parsons, Ian, *A Marriage of True Minds* (London, 1977)

Stansky, Peter, and Abrahams, William, *Journey to the Frontier: Julian Bell and John Cornford; their lives and the 1930's* (London, 1966)

Woolf, Leonard, *An Autobiography* (5 vols, London, 1960–73)

Woolf, Virginia, *Diary*, ed. Anne Olivier Bell (5 vols, London, 1977–84)

— *Letters*, ed. Nigel Nicolson (6 vols, London, 1975–80)

— *Moments of Being*, ed. Jeanne Schulkind (new ed., London, 1978)

— *A Writer's Diary* (London, 1953)

SOME OTHER FIGURES ASSOCIATED WITH CHARLESTON

Ackroyd, Peter, *T. S. Eliot* (London, 1984)

Carrington, Dora, *Carrington: Letters and Extracts from her Diaries*, ed. David Garnett (London, 1970)

DeSalvo, Louise & Leaska, Mitchell, eds, *The Letters of Vita Sackville-West to Virginia Woolf* (London, 1984)

Edel, Leon, *Bloomsbury: A House of Lions* (London, 1979)

Fielding, Xan, ed., *Best of Friends: The Brenan-Partridge Letters* (London, 1986)

Forster, E. M., *Selected Letters*, ed. Mary Lago and P. N. Furbank (2 vols, London, 1983, 1985)

Furbank, P. N., *E. M. Forster: A Life* (Oxford, 1979)

Gadd, David, *The Loving Friends* (London, 1974)

Glendinning, Victoria, *Vita* (London, 1983)

Keynes, Milo, ed., *Lydia Lopokova* (London, 1983)

Lehmann, John, *The Whispering Gallery* (London, 1955)

Partridge, Frances, *Everything to Lose: Diaries, 1945-60* (London, 1985)

— *Friends in Focus* (London, 1987)

— *Memories* (London, 1981)

— *A Pacifist's War* (London, 1978)

List of Illustrations